"This work is a treasure—reverent, touching and timely. It echoes the wisdom of the scriptures: *Ask the beasts to teach you, and the birds of the air to tell you, or the reptiles on earth to instruct you and the fish of the sea to inform you* (Job 12: 7-9). A book to pray rather than read—I highly recommend it."

Macrina Wiederkehr
Author, *The Song of the Seed*

"This 'supernatural geographic' invites the reader–prayer to see more and more deeply into and then beyond the attractive metaphors of grace which have invited the author to stop, look and listen. Father Fitzgerald shares with us again his reverence for God in the divine indwelling which resides in the shells of snails, the fur of grizzlies and the wings of one hundred cranes. After reading this unique book, one finds oneself walking more and more gently, watching more caringly, resting more actively and praising the Creator a little more sensefully. Eat well at this table of prayer which Father Fitzgerald has set before those of us who have eyes to see and ears to hear."

Larry Gillick, S.J.
Professor, Creighton University

"In this enchanting book, Father Bill achieves what many of us might have thought was impossible in this day and age. By exploring our lives through those of animals and plants—matching our struggles with theirs—he carries us out of the confusion and clutter of the world we have constructed to where the simple joy of living can illuminate us. Drawing upon insights from distant times and cultures as well as his own encounters with the natural world, Father Bill shows us a world immeasurably rich, with many levels of meaning."

Susan Lamb
Naturalist, Author, *The Smithsonian Guide to Natural America*

"*One Hundred Cranes* gives a lyrical, sensitive and profound awareness of our interconnectedness with all creation. It will nourish the soul with the healing necessary in this turbulent, uncertain world."

Mary Jan Benton
Essentially Books

"*One Hundred Cranes* evokes in us memories of beauty and the experience of enchantment; the sacred comes alive as we read this delightful and imaginative book. Bill Fitzgerald helps us discover our true self and realize on a deep level that every creature of the Earth Community is cousin to each other. *One Hundred Cranes* is a powerful panorama of wisdom, passion and hope; truly a prayer book for our time!"

Jim Conlan

Author, *Geo-Justice: a Preferential Option for the Earth; Lyrics for Re-Creation*. Director, *Institute in Culture and Creation Spirituality*

"Father Fitzgerald has created a uniquely beautiful and inspirational collection of meditations which allow all who read them to at once enjoy a new closeness to nature and to God. *One Hundred Cranes* is an intimate journey to the heart of God's creation with the power to let the reader feel the beating of the heart of the creator.

For all in search of a deeper insight into the purpose of creation and the role intended for each of us, *One Hundred Cranes* is a much sought after guide."

John Cavanaugh

former U.S. Congressman; present Chairman of the Platte River Critical Habitat Maintainance Trust

"Father Fitzgerald's poetry and prose in *One Hundred Cranes* inspired me and provided for me the spiritual connection I feel to God's universe each time I visit the Platte River at the time of the sandhill crane migration."

Kate Cavanaugh

Omaha World columnist and author of *Pete Goes to Grand Island*, a book on the sandhill crane migration

COVER ART AND ILLUSTRATIONS BY
DUFFI GOODRICH

One hundred Cranes

Praying with the Chorus of Creation

William J. Fitzgerald

Foreword by Joyce Rupp, O.S.M.

FOREST OF PEACE
PUBLISHING

Suppliers for the Spiritual Pilgrim

Also by the Author:
(available through the publisher)

Seasons of the Earth and Heart

One Hundred Cranes

copyright © 1996, by William J. Fitzgerald

Library of Congress Cataloging-in-Publication Data

Fitzgerald, William , 1932
    One hundred cranes : praying with the chorus of creation / William J. Fitzgerald ; foreword by Joyce Rupp.
        p.   cm.
    ISBN 0-939516-31-4
    1. Animals--Religious aspects--Meditations.   2. Plants--Religious aspects--Meditations.   I. Title.
    BL325.A6F58   1996
    291.4'3--dc20

                                        96-11900   ´
                                            CIP

published by

Forest of Peace Publishing, Inc.
PO Box 269
Leavenworth, KS 66048-0269 USA
1-800-659-3227

printed by

Hall Directory, Inc.
Topeka, KS 66608-0348

illustrations by

Duffi Goodrich

1st printing: May 1996

Dedication

to my golden retriever, Joe, companion of my youth,
and to the cranes,
messengers of the holy

With Special Appreciation to

Duffi Goodrich,
my collaborator,
for telling the story of these creatures
in her illustrations,
an integral part of this book

Diane Cummings-Halle of the Cummings Foundation

Former U.S. Rep. John and Kate Cavanaugh,
who led me to the cranes

My parents, Bill and Kitty,
who led me to
"thin places"
where wild creatures abound

And to Jackie, Marj and Ken, Kathy, Mick, Laura, Joan, Val,
Susan, Joyce, Larry, Tony, Jack and Ed in the U.S.
and Mary in Ireland,
who journeyed with me
through the magic forest

In Memoriam:

Fr. Jim Fitzgerald and Ken Kunce,
seekers and catchers of the great
"Salmon of Knowledge"

TABLE OF CONTENTS

Foreword

For as long as I can remember I have believed that the creatures of the universe are my teachers. As a child on a farm I spent a lot of time alone with the earth, at first playing in the grove and then, as I grew older, working with the animals and the land. I felt a oneness with creation that has never left me. To this day the smell of newly cut grass takes me back immediately to the early mornings when I would walk out to the pasture and smell the freshly mown alfalfa. There was a sense of a presence much greater than myself as I felt my spirit lift with the freshness of the fields.

As I helped to work the land, I constantly received wisdom from all I saw and experienced. I observed how animals cared for their young, how earth—when readied and opened—received seeds graciously, how winter's howl never lasted forever, how the gathering in of the harvest gave a mellowness and a fullness to my heart as I saw the results of all our hard work. These many things that I beheld in my early years only became wisdoms later in my life when I paused to reflect on the teachings of my time with the earth.

There is a presence among the created things of God which draws me ever and always to the transcendent. When I was a teenager I used to come home at night after school activities and stand at the window in my bedroom, gazing at the stars. I often felt mezmerized by them. Standing with the stars felt much like being with my brothers and sisters of the sky. I had few words to say to God in those days, but I knew as I stood there in the night that I was forever and always connected to a gracious Creator. I found comfort and hope in those star-filled times.

Always I am both humbled and awed by the universe and all who abide there. Thus, as I read *One Hundred Cranes* I was overjoyed. William Fitzgerald has captured secrets of the unknown ones, spoken for the creatures, bridged them to our lives and given us wisdoms that I will long carry within me. His poetic approach, his keen inner eye of beauty and his creative storytelling have the power to bring us in touch again with the mystery of God and the wonder of creation.

One Hundred Cranes reminds me of what Teilhard de Chardin wrote so many years ago in his *Hymn of the Universe*:

> ...never will you be able to say to matter, "I have seen enough of you; I have surveyed your mysteries and have taken from them enough food for my thoughts to last me forever." I tell you: even though like the Sage of sages, you carried in your memory the image of all the beings that people the earth or swim in the seas, still all that knowledge would be as nothing for your soul...this is because to understand the world knowledge is not enough, you must see it, touch it, live in its presence....

William Fitzgerald has done just that—he has taken us in spirit to be with the mystery of creation. He has flown with the cranes, swum with the salmon, crawled with the snail and sat with the tortoise. He invites us to do the same: to see, touch and live in the sacred presence of matter through these and many other creatures. Each page of *One Hundred Cranes* offers an opportunity to nourish our souls and to approach all of life with awe and reverence. Enter into these stories and prayers and find wisdom for your lives.

Joyce Rupp, O.S.M.

Introduction

PRAYERS FOR ALL TIMES AND SEASONS

Awe and wonder are the beginnings of prayer. I believe my prayer and this book may have begun when I was four years old and glimpsed a wondrous and unique bird. Many years later I now believe that all of God's creatures can call us to prayer. In the following pages, I hope that the reflections about birds, animals and plants might create a mood for your own prayers.

My first religious experience of an awe-inspiring bird stands out like an engraved etching among the vague recollections of early childhood. For me it is a revelatory image that tells a story and holds within it many questions.

The year was 1936 when I had my once-in-a-lifetime glimpse of an alien creature from an almost forgotten world. When it dipped out of April's rain-laden clouds, my small eyes widened into saucers. Was I seeing a stork? Was it bringing a baby brother or sister? No, it was not a stork. It was an ancient crane bringing a rare presence and a survivor's story.

Snowy white with a red cap, its long neck extended forward and its fluted, black-tipped wings flared back like multiple victory pennants. It flew with spindly crane legs drooping behind like afterthoughts. Now I know what I could not know at such an early age. The bird was a whooping crane. In 1936, it was only one of 29 survivors of a vanishing species.

The Crane—A Symbol for Our Time

The story of the whooping crane is the first story in this book because the unique saga of the whoopers' struggle to survive as a species has caught the attention of many and has reminded us of how wonderful and precious are all God's creatures. In its fragility and its numinosity the whooping crane provides a needed symbol for a spirituality of creation that rekindles human reverence for the mysterious presence of God dwelling deep down within the beauty and splendor of all that lives.

Their Species' Stories—A Prayer Presence

This book contains stories, reflections and prayers based on the elegance, beauty and evolving mystery of birds such as the cranes, as well as of other animals, fish and plants. It recognizes our fundamental unity with them on planet earth.

Their stories are in some sense our stories too. Their ancestors were here long before ours! They prepared the way for humans. By meditating on their stories, we can enter into an attitude of wonder, leading to awe, gratitude and reflective prayer.

This book is meant to sharpen your awareness of the wonderfully diverse species that share our planet. Their very presence in our imaginations can stir a sense of prayer. Their graceful movements hint of a divine energy. Their sometimes comical behavior points toward a humorous creator. Their splendid diversity and complex evolution reveal a divinely creative imagination. Their adaptations in the face of great obstacles can stimulate our own hope-filled prayer.

Prayer Moods

The following chapters are arranged so that they relate to various human moods, dispositions and life experiences. They could be read and used straight through, or the chapters could be chosen according to your particular prayer needs at a given time in your life experience. Each segment is meant to create a prayer mood which can open a door for your own reflection, personal prayer or journaling.

Each series of prayer experiences is introduced by a personal experience or nature story taken from my own journal or from that of a friend. With only two exceptions, I have encountered each of the creatures written about in this book. These meetings have always been blessings. It is hoped that you too will be blessed by meeting and praying with these creatures of sky, earth and water.

Chapter One

Praying with the Whooping Crane,
Mythic Cranes
and Sandhill Cranes

Prayers for Survival and the Dance of Life

Praying with the Whooping Crane

All other environmental problems pale beside the ongoing
extinction crisis...if we let too many species go, we face an
enormous psychological and spiritual loss.

> E. O. Wilson, Harvard Sociobiologist, "Living
> With Nature," *U.S. News & World Report*

The whooping crane I encountered in my childhood came out of
the hazy dawn of antiquity, and its flight path plummeted toward
zero and oblivion. Even then, my childish instincts hinted to me
that I was seeing an amazing and unique creature, something I
had not seen before, and might never see again.

The whooping crane is the tallest of American birds; when
standing it can measure four and a half feet. Its ancestors thus
made large targets for the gunners of the western frontier. In the
nineteenth century its forebears were ravaged like the bison. In
the twentieth century its species faced the fate of the dinosaurs,
not from cataclysmic upheavals, but from the "dominion" of
mankind. In its stark loneliness, the whooping crane flew into the
twentieth century bearing a story filled with challenging questions.

One question might well be: "Does human dominion bestow
the right to ravage beauty and to create loneliness on planet earth?"
As countless species disappear, the earth surely becomes less diverse
and more devoid of potential. Massive extinctions replace

blessings with a curse. Is the red mark on the head of the whooping crane like the death stain of Cain? Does it symbolize the decree of death for any creature that seems to get in the way of humankind's "progress"?

Or might the cranes' struggle for survival and the human sympathy it has engendered signal a new awakening to a spirituality that reverences creation? Might it remind us to be the stewards of earth who nurture its splendid diversity, and thus pay homage to a wise creator?

In our unique time and season, could the eons-long drama of the crane played out in the heavens enliven our diminished imaginations? Could it not deepen our sense of holy connectedness with extravagant and surprising beauty? Would we not be wise to heed its spiritual presence, just as Noah reverenced the bird bearing the leaf?

One Hundred Cranes

The story of the whooping cranes and the questions their plight raises regarding the extinction of species were first considered only by a few, but then by more and more concerned humans. In 1937, just one year after my own sighting of a whooping crane, President Franklin Roosevelt signed an executive order declaring over 47,000 acres in south Texas as a wildlife preserve. This presidential order was an eleventh-hour reprieve for the whooping crane. At 11:59 P.M. and counting toward midnight execution, twenty-nine whooping cranes, the last of their species, were given a chance to live.

From that point on, their dramatic story is documented. A year later, they were up to thirty-five. Year by year their numbers fluctuated. In 1944 they diminished to twenty-one. After that another increase, only to hit the low-water mark of twenty-one again in 1953. Then there was a gradual yearly increase. Each year this tiny but growing remnant would trek from Texas to their subarctic nesting grounds in the Northwest Territories, a journey of over twenty-five hundred miles. There, on harsh terrain, a few precious eggs would be tended. This would be followed by a migration of heroic proportions. On a return flight to Texas, one whooping crane family, two parents and their offspring, was clocked flying one thousand and eighty-six miles nonstop from South Dakota to Texas!

In 1983, twenty-nine years after the low-water census for the cranes, the one hundredth whooping crane was born in the dangerously exposed nesting grounds in Canada. There can be a moment in any heroic effort when victory or defeat hangs in the balance. For the human marathoner it may come at the moment of the second wind. For the eons-long flights of the whooping cranes, it may have come with the survival of the one hundredth crane.

The Cranes' Struggles—and Ours

The cranes have struggled to survive against great and cruel odds. Could their ordeal be a "writing in the sky," an omen of the human struggles to survive "ethnic cleansings," holocausts and other demonic "final solutions" devised on earth below?

Can the threat to such a noble bird remind us of our own "extinctions"—the plight of innocent victims, the erosion of jobs and futures, the countless daily losses, subtractions and wounds that diminish our human spirits? In the face of all this, can their indomitable flight lift up our prayers and our hearts?

PRAYING WITH ONE HUNDRED CRANES
FOR BETTER DREAMS

We and those we love face the extinctions
    of empty nests, severed mates,
    obsolete employments, smothered dreams.
There are put-downs and shutdowns,
    shot down dreams,
    and wounded wings that barely fly.

What of your flight, ancient cranes?
    Like the Light Brigade, you plummet through volleys of death.
You are the stubborn survivors of whooping flocks
    holding out in sandhill sloughs.
Your spring muster is not at all like Custer's,
    but more like Bastogne's "Nuts! We shall not surrender!"

Divine Maker of ancient votive cranes,
    Creative Source of their evolutionary saga—and ours—
    Final Cause of all allurement,
    light one hundred candles in the sky.
Give flight to our hopes,
    and tend our fragile dreams.

Image: The majestic and rare whooping crane, long-necked, red-capped, sparkling white with black-fluted wings. See it soar out of a stormy cloud, like some long forgotten dream. Pray for your own and your loved ones' dreams.

Journal: The heroic survival of the whooping crane moves me to...

Praying with Mythic Cranes

People claim the land by creating sacred sites, by mythologizing the animals and plants.

Joseph Campbell, *The Power of Myth*

The cranes in flight, long necks silhouetted against a half-lit sky, present a spectral, otherworldly image. Like Star Trekkers, sifting through the night mists, they seem to emerge from another time, a far-off place, delivering messages from some ancient prehuman wisdom. Storytellers through the ages have observed their flight and have been moved to spin their yarns. In "Paradise Lost," John Milton marveled at their ancient and ordered presence in the sky, describing them as an "airy caravan."

Flying not only out of the everyday world of sunrise and sunset, but also out of the enchanted tales of mythmakers, cranes have found their way into the legends and imagery of cultures as distant and different as Greece, Ireland and Japan. In all of these legends they deliver a message to humans.

Greek Crane Mythology

There is an ancient Greek myth dating to the year 550 B.C. It is about a man attacked by robbers near Corinth and left to die on the road. As he lay dying, a flock of cranes flew over, and he begged them to avenge his death. Some time after his death, when the murderer was at an outdoor amphitheater, a flock of cranes appeared and hovered over his head. In fright, he cried out, "The cranes of Ibycus, my avengers!" In this way, he revealed his own murderous identity, and he and the other robbers were exposed. Perhaps in our own time, the cranes of Ibycus hover over humankind and accuse us of robbing and plundering the earth.

The Greek poet Homer told of an ancient myth about a race of pygmies who feared the cranes' spring arrival and made war with them to avoid losing some of the tribe's grain. Could this same myth be applied to our own time? Are not we humans of the twentieth century too often small-minded? Don't we let our narrow self-interest and midget vision interfere with making room for all of God's creatures on planet earth?

IRISH FOLKLORE

In iconography, angels have been depicted as winged creatures from another world. This is in accord with the thought of ancient Celts, for they believed that winged creatures—ravens, swans, cranes—were especially related to the "Other World." Caitlin Matthews suggests in *The Celtic Tradition* that more than any culture the Celts valued otherworldly states of consciousness. For them, birds were most associated with mystical adventures and consolations. As an example, the singing of the birds of Rhiannon caused battle-weary warriors to lose any sense of time and space. In Celtic pagan lore human beings could also be turned into birds and fly to the Other World. Oengus, as a young God, was visited by a dream-woman, and they ended up flying away as two white birds.

Viewing cranes as otherworldly would come quite easily to the Celts, for cranes' long necks and spindly legs make them appear eerie and spectral in the mists of Ireland. Even when birds appeared as creatures out of divine visions, underlying all Celtic myths was the close kinship these ancient peoples had with otherworldly creatures.

COLUMBA AND THE CRANE

In the Christian era that spirit of kinship was carried on by the renowned sixth century Irish missionary, Columba, while in self-exile on the isle of Iona. The visit of an exhausted crane called forth the hospitality any good host would extend to a weary and distinguished traveller who arrived as a guest at the door. Columba felt that a visitor as majestic as the crane deserved generous hospitality, and so he instructed one of his brethren thus:

> On the third day from this that is breaking, thou oughtest to sit on the seashore, and look out in the western part of this island for from the northern part of Ireland a certain guest, a crane to wit, beaten by the winds during long and circuitous aerial flights, will arrive after the ninth hour of the day...Thou will take care to lift it up tenderly, and carry it to some neighboring house.[1]

Columba ensured that this crane would be received as a noble ambassador from his native land—to be fed, nurtured and healed so that it might return to "its former sweet home in Ireland."

JAPANESE CRANE LORE

When Kumiko and Ikuko, two nineteen-year-old visitors from Japan came to our city, they presented me with a gift of paper cranes. Each of the paper cranes was carefully folded with the distinctive neck and head thrusting forward. When I asked them the significance of the cranes, they told me that at Hiroshima, one of the two cities destroyed by atomic bombs in World War II, there is a beautiful statue of a girl who died from leukemia caused by atomic radiation from the blast. Kumiko smiled when describing that revered statue and went on to explain that Sadako was a little girl when the atomic bomb was dropped. Suffering from the effects of radiation, she folded paper cranes hoping that they would augur good health again. According to Japanese legend, folding one thousand cranes would make a wish come true. After her death, her classmates completed the 356 cranes she had not finished. Visitors to the Hiroshima Peace Park drape paper cranes around her statue. Each paper crane is now a prayer for peace in the world. In the statue's hand rests a golden crane. Engraved below the statue are the words:

> This is our cry,
> this is our prayer;
> peace in the world.

The story of Sadako has been immortalized by Eleanor Coerr in her book *Sadako and the Thousand Paper Cranes*—a new chapter in Japanese crane lore. Our two Japanese visitors told us this story on the exact forty-sixth anniversary of the World War II atomic bombing at Nagasaki. They told it as they visited our city which was then the headquarters of the Strategic Air Command responsible for the bombing. They told it in the city whose bomber factory constructed the Enola Gay, the plane that dropped the bomb.

When they finished their story, there was a long silence. All of us present realized the synchronicity of their crane story told on the anniversary of that mushroom clouded event so long ago.

THE MESSAGES OF CRANES

We asked for more stories about the significance of the cranes. "Oh, there are many," they replied. "The Japan Airlines plane we traveled on had the symbol of the crane as its logo. No wonder, since there are so many stories of cranes carrying other small creatures on their backs. There are also tales of soldiers slain in battle being borne up to heaven on the wings of cranes." As we listened, it struck me again that the Oriental crane myths bear a resemblance to our western angel stories, tales of winged creatures bringing messages and help into the lives of humans.

One tale they shared with us has been passed down from generation to generation and was told to them as little children. It began as all good stories do:

Once upon a time, a farmer trudging home through the snow, discovered a crane trapped and unable to fly. He released it, and it flew away. That night, the farmer and his wife were visited by a beautiful young girl who sought shelter from a raging storm. They took her in and allowed her to stay and join their family.

After awhile, the newly adopted daughter offered to weave some cloth for them. They accepted her offer. After days of weaving in her room, she presented them with a beautiful tapestry which she suggested they sell for gold.

Soon, the fine cloth was sold for an abundant return. The young maiden continued to weave, but always in private. One day the old mother could not contain her curiosity any longer so she peeked into the room. To her great surprise, she discovered a beautiful white crane at the loom weaving her own feathers into new cloth. When recognized, the crane disappeared, declaring: "Your discovering that I am really the crane you once rescued and set free allows me to return from whence I came." And so the crane set free by kindness flew away into the sky.

MESSENGERS OF GOD

In *The Golden Crane*, Tohr Yamaguchi recalls a similar ancient tale of a boy and his stepfather befriending a wounded crane. Since people had never seen such a crane up close, they gazed on it with admiration. One was moved to exclaim, "This holy bird speaks the message of God!"

The tale ends with the child and the old man who befriended the crane being lifted up on cranes' wings and borne aloft. Perhaps the ancient belief that soldiers were carried to heaven on the wings of cranes derives from this ancient story.

Listening to these wonderful crane stories told by our Japanese guests, it became apparent to us that the Japanese people pass down through the ages a rich crane lore that becomes an enduring symbol of hope and transformation for their children. Thus the mythic cranes become "the messengers of God."

PRAYING WITH THE MYTHIC CRANES
FOR OUR CHILDRENS' FUTURE

Holy Creator of all that is,
we thank you for your messengers, the cranes,
images of grace,
bringers of peace.

Noble couriers, long-necked and alert,
red-capped porters of antiquities,
making their monumental treks
for millions of years.

From Nippon to Siberia,
from warm gulf to subarctic,
carriers of myths and fables,
omens and portents in the sky.

Sentinels of unfolding seasons,
hauling and hurling winter after fall,
gently lifting spring northwards,
mystical winds of heaven, holy birds.

May their hovering over polluted rivers,
plowed and blowing sandhills,
alert us, accuse us, arouse us
and cast shadows over greed and glut.

Deliver us, O God, from a midget vision
of living simply for today,
forgetting yesterdays,
scorning our childrens' tomorrows.

Form in us a cranelike vision,
an endurance for the long haul.
May your message in the sky inspire us
and bear our children on wings of promise.

"This is our cry,
this is our prayer;
       peace in the world."
       The cry of the cranes.

Image: Children and the cranes. See children from every nation placing paper cranes on the statue in Japan. Pray for the future of children and grandchildren you know.

Journal: The cranes of Ibycus remind me...

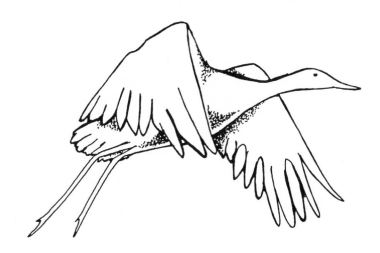

PRAYING WITH THE SANDHILL CRANE

Both breathtaking and mysterious...one of the world's most magnificent wildlife spectacles—spring arrival of the cranes on the Platte...it is often compared to the majestic wildlife migration on the African Serengeti.

Fred Thomas, National Audubon Society, "Nebraska Sky Full of Cranes," *Omaha World Herald*, March 4, 1994

Along the Platte valley in Nebraska, the ides of March beckon large numbers of sandhill cranes, cousins of the whoopers, to come, to feed and rest awhile before continuing their migrations, some as far as Siberia. They also summon viewers from around the world.

Fifty years passed between my childhood sighting of a lone whooping crane and my own visit to see thousands of its cousins, the sandhill cranes. I joined a young congressman and others interested in the preservation of the Platte River wetlands on an expedition to the resting place of the cranes on the Platte.

Getting up at three o'clock in the morning, we trooped toward the Morman Lake Sanctuary near Grand Island. Our walk took us to a bunker where we could observe the cranes without bothering them.

We waited for dawn. When the sun began to peer over the river, its reflection was like an outpouring of molten gold from a black refiner's bucket. It splashed across the wide and shallow river. Trees, willows and cranes were black silhouettes on the shimmering water. Eagles perched across the river. A flock of wild turkeys stirred on tree limbs, and thousands of cranes stood knee-deep in the safe water shallows. The sight was close to perfect. Rightly so, for this engraving upon gold had been in process for millions of years.

The cranes we viewed were some of the half-million sandhill cranes who funnel their flight path into the narrow Platte River staging area. As the sun emerged, they rose up in immense flocks from the river bottoms, creating a cacophony of sound like the rising and rolling roar from a wildly clapping audience. Long beaks and necks stretched forward. Spindly legs trailed behind as though stretching back into other millennia. (Crane fossils predating human history have been found in this area near the Platte.) It was as if a curtain had been pulled back on that prehistory. The sight was haunting.

RED-CAP COUSINS

These cousins of the whoopers bear the distinctive red caps of the whoopers, but their feathers are a brownish gray. At their peak Nebraska arrival time in March and April, nearly eighty percent of all the sandhill cranes in the world will gather along a fifty-mile stretch of the Platte near Grand Island. Visitors come from around the world to glimpse this wildlife spectacle.

A DANCE TO THE JOY OF LIFE

Each spring, the cranes dance at the Platte. Before the country-western line dances in Grand Island, before the Native American war dances, before the waltz in Vienna, before David danced around the ark, before the cave men and women danced around their fires, the cranes have performed their intricate mating dances at the Platte. Feet askew, they leap straight up in the air, their large wing spans forming a V shape. Through this dance, they choose one mate for life. It is a stirring, primeval pageant.

What human movements can compare to it? The sensuous tango? The victory jig? Perhaps both. But a better comparison might be that of a child who without any coaching breaks into a spontaneous skip. Perhaps skipping was the first human dance of joy. However, millennia before it ever occurred the cranes took the lead in the dance to the joy of life.

Could the cranes teach us to dance to life rather than flirt with death? The cranes, like most creatures, claim territory and sometimes fuss and fight about it, but they do not attempt to kill their cousins, the whoopers, in the process. Only members of species such as the praying mantis, the human and some others kill their relatives.

Each spring, in Hall County, Nebraska, the sandhill cranes return peacefully to their familiar haunts. Near the Platte River is a stone marker dating to a more recent migration. The cranes surround it, serenely feeding on the nutrients that give them strength for their long journey. The inscription on the marker reads:

> In 1864, at this spot, 1/2 mile from the Martinville Stage
> office, two brothers, Nathaniel and Ray Martin, were struck
> by two Indian arrows which pinned the two boys together.

The Indians apparently won this skirmish, but later were violently moved from this lush valley to the Dakota reservations. Like the whooping cranes and the buffalo, they too almost met extinction.

Only in our time have the Indians been granted the full rights of citizenship. Only in our own time too have we begun to strike a truce with the cranes. No other river in the United States supplies as much water for irrigation as the Platte. Through conservation projects for the wetlands, a truce must be forged to save the Platte for all its tenants including its most ancient ones, the cranes.

CROSSROADS

Each spring, the cranes' south-north migratory path stretches from as far north as Siberia all the way south to Mexico. Here at the Platte, it crisscrosses the historic paths of east-west human migrations—the pioneers' Overland Trail, the first transcontinental railroad and today's Interstate 80. At this crossroads, death and life have intersected. Here the slaughter of buffalo meant death for the lifestyle of the plains Indians and a threat to their deepest spirituality. The Native Americans had a mystic, relational kinship with the buffalo, the cranes and all other creatures. They included "all their relatives" in prayer. Something deeply spiritual was erased when the white man destroyed the buffalo. The meaning of a sacred place and a holy encounter between the Native Americans and their "relatives" was extinguished. To reduce such meaning is to diminish life.

In this valley of the Platte, there has been a collision between a right of way acquired over millennia and the human expansion of the last one hundred years. So far, the cranes have survived, and each spring, more and more visitors come to watch them dance and in doing so are spiritually uplifted.

CRANES AND THE PLATTE

At the Platte, the cranes gain energy in the spring for their nesting flight to the north, and in the fall for their flight of renewal to the gulf coast. Paired for life, they soar above without the aid of radar, but equipped with an instinctual "road map" fine-tuned through the ages.

They fly above the seasons of human discontent—not far from Offutt Air Force Base, whose eagle's nest once possessed the red telephone and the atomic button. They also fly close to a low waste nuclear dump "awarded" to the State of Nebraska. They sometimes alight near toxic chemicals hurtling by on the Union Pacific main line. They are birds of life skirting the human boundaries of death.

Their flight seems right, their joyful dance along the Platte an avian ode to life and joy. By comparison, the flight of the human species sometimes seems to be a lemmings' quest towards death. Could the cranes teach us to dance?

ODE TO THE SANDHILL

On a March day in 1991 the temperature in the Platte Valley reached 80 degrees; forty-eight hours later a spring blizzard roared out of the west shutting down Interstate 80 for six hours! In the midst of it all, the cranes held steady.

The suddenly shifting jet stream
turns spring zephyrs into slushy snow.
It stalls semitrailers and pins down tourists
but does not deter the cranes at all.
They ride the crests of howling winds,
veering in toward land—trusting the Platte.
Like the first commandos from landing crafts,
they stand in the icy waters.
Their orange eyes flash "Caution!"

Crafty eagles, like snipers,
peer down from nude branches,
ever alert for the straggler,
the faltering weakest link.
And then the capricious March wind
shifts and strips away the snowy skies,
as though flinging back a bed sheet.
The setting sun throws a bold streak of rouge
against the yawning Nebraska sky.
Surprising beauty flares across emptiness.
White-robed sandhills unfold down to the Platte.
The wetlands exhale a steamy mist.
The cranes stand still.
This too shall pass and return.
And so shall they.

Prayer for Finding Our Way

Holy One:

Fix in our minds and hearts the image of the cranes
as they journey through the ages,
through millennia of shifting ice
and emerging plains,
from the swampy marshes
toward the azure heavens.
May we likewise find our instinct
for the right way to go,
the right time,
the best place.

May we share their endurance,
their graceful movement
and their undiminished spirits
in our own spring crossings and transformations,
in our desert times,
our coming home, and going out,
our hard frozen times,
our rejoicing and flights of fancy times.

Just as they are fine-tuned
to the pull and push of life,
and the bliss of their sky path,
may we find our own way,
and dance with them,
to the joy of life.

Image: The cranes taking off from the icy waters of the Platte—I pray that I too may soar and...

Journal: Following my bliss may mean...

Chapter Two

Praying with the Snail,
Salmon
and Wild Geese

Prayers for Spring Crossings and Transformations

Praying with the Snail

550 million years ago: invention of the shell by the snail...first encounter of snails and humans: 2.6 million years ago.

Brian Swimme and Thomas Berry,
The Universe Story

There can be certain times in our lives when energies converge. We encounter unique transit points when we pass over to something new. Such critical moments elicit our full attention. They give us the feeling of being fully alive, alert to every signal and sensation. The runner in the ninth inning of the World Series breaks for home on a three-two pitch. A young person completes a successful interview for a first job. A chemically dependent person takes the first of twelve steps out of chaos. A mother hears her newborn shriek and suck in the first breath. Moments of birth, rebirth and renewal elicit our attention. They might even provide us with hints of an ultimate human transcendence.

These moments are so electrifying they wake us up. They might help us to become aware that a lot of times we are just sleepwalking through life. This can often be true with our relationship to the planet and the universe. Our awareness of the mysterious life and energy all around us in the cosmos is easily diminished. How long has it been since you received a signal from a star? In most metro areas, the stars are invisible. When did you stand in the holy dark? It is difficult to do since we are so often bathed in artificial light. We are all the more cut off from most of the creatures of the animal and plant world. We miss so much of the drama and beauty of creation that goes on beyond our backyard fences and concrete towers.

And then, if we are fortunate, we experience a special encounter. We move beyond our normal limits. Paths cross. We connect and we feel a sense of being more alive in a wondrous world.

Point Reyes

Such a crossing took place for me and a friend on a sparkling spring day at Point Reyes, just north of San Francisco. Both of us were at transit points in our own lives. We had just finished the final semester in a graduate program in Creation Spirituality. We were not sure of the details of what would come next. I would be heading eastward, and she would return to the Midwest for what she described as "challenge, risk, wisdom...." I was fifty-five; she was forty-seven. We had been classmates and friends, and now our class was about to disperse, with each of us going our separate ways.

We decided we would take one of our last days to do "the San Francisco tourist thing." We wanted to sense for one last time the cream-colored city necklaced by the blue bay. We did. We rode the cable car through Chinatown. We were hushed at Muir Woods. We took in Fisherman's Wharf and scouted the seals at the Cliff House.

As the afternoon sun began to wane, we headed north across the Golden Gate and up the north coast to Point Reyes, a lighthouse whose jaw jutted out toward China. That twilight visit was so remarkable for me that every detail floods back as a mellow memory. As we walked toward the lighthouse, we paused at a promontory point. We overlooked the green undulating hills. Their valley shadows were like the pointed tips of black velvet gloves fingering the sea. Looking northward, it seemed we could gaze up a sandy corridor all the way to Oregon. The ocean waves rippled and unfurled like the stripes of an endless flag. There were no human beings visible on the beach below.

It was a rare moment when we sensed how wonderful it is to be fully alive and attentive to the unspoiled beauty flooding into our senses. At that moment, a most unexpected creature appeared before us. It was the largest snail I have ever seen. Its movement was not even perceptible on the path in front of us. My friend was fascinated by the sight. "Where did it come from? How did it arrive on this cliffside? Where is it going? How will it ever get there?" These were the questions we shared about the snail, but in retrospect they were also questions about ourselves at that transit point in our lives.

As we continued along the path, three deer peeked their heads over the crown of a hill speckled with waving yellow poppies. They were not more than twenty feet away. Their cocked ears and quizzical eyes seemed to say, "And just what are you doing here?"

Suddenly, there appeared above us a beautiful falcon. It seemed suspended in space. It was riding a rising wave of warm air, and for a few moments it remained motionless on that thermal, as though posing for a still picture. It then curved off and rose higher above the breaking waves below.

We reached the lighthouse and peered beyond the rail. A distant freighter edged toward the rim of the horizon and dipped into the crimson twilight. When we looked down below us, we encountered our fourth species of creature within ten minutes. A marvelous gray whale was effortlessly swimming and spouting at the point.

In this compressed period of time, all of these creatures— the human, the whale, the deer, the falcon and the snail—had crossed paths, each on their own journey, but each sharing the tides, the sun and the earth. At that sunset moment, we felt a deep kinship with all of them.

When we returned along the path, the snail had vanished! It had seemed to have been moving at an infinitesimally slow pace, and yet it had passed over and was gone. We mused about the snail, about slowing down, about savoring every moment of every day of our journeys.

The Ultimate Transits—Death and Transcendence

After that day, we parted. She went on home seeking a new life. Two months later on an August afternoon, on her way to a job interview, she crossed an intersection—a transit point. A drunk driver did not slow down. He careened through a red light and drove aimlessly into the side of my friend's car, killing her instantly.

Leaping Beyond

As I look back now on that special day we shared at the ocean, I see it as a *grace filled* moment. I realize that the creatures we met graced us by awakening us. It was a vision of life-forms gracefully fulfilling all that their instincts called them to be.

They jolted us from the daily trance of self-absorption. They lifted our eyes beyond a narrow view. Their presence prompted us to ponder the meaning of such extravagant beauty. And they challenged our unique human gift to dream even beyond the horizon of such a splendid day.

On that day, we experienced creation like a pregnant woman, blooming and filled with promise. And beneath our feet in the unexpected snail, there was an immanence of glory and a whisper of transcendence.

Perhaps the first hints of transcendence might be seen in any creature's amazing gracefulness in passing a transit point—

and accomplishing far more than we would have any reason to expect. By what logic should a snail reach the heights where we found it—or even at its pace, succeed in arriving anywhere?

And the other creatures we met—a deep and marvelous instinct impelled those creatures to crawl, to breach, to leap, to soar and fulfill their destinies. Some inner spark from the original fireball hurled down through eons of evolution fired them toward their full potential. When I ponder their graceful movements, I am reminded of an inner human stirring, a dynamism that nudges us humans toward being more than we could ever dream—even as we seem to be plodding along, simply making our way. Call it a human instinct for transcendence. Buried deep within us a spark of springtime yearns and pines to leap up even beyond the cold boundaries of death.

Somehow, I believe that if that snail could pass over toward a splendid sunset and a gracious arrival...so has my friend.

A Creature's Passage Prayer

A mighty leviathan roams the sea,
its pace measured by leagues,
>   furrowing, diving, reigning majestically,
>   spouting geysers of jubilee.

The freed-up falcon rides the thermal,
its pace measured by its whims,
>   suspended in time and flight,
>   coasting above land and sea.

The fleet deer jumps beyond limits,
its pace measured by leaps and bounds,
>   antlered escape artist,
>   soaring past human constraints.

The snail passes over a transit point,
its mpace measured by staying the course,
>   not arriving by any fleet movement
>   but by being present to every moment.

My Transformation Prayer Through Loss and Grief

Sacred Source and End of All That Is:
awaken my spirit to immanent glory,
>   and stirrings of transcendence.
>   Guide my path toward beauty and its source.

Deliver me from crazed red-light hit-men
and from yellow-light poachers.
>   Lift my numbed spirit from whir and blur,
>   hours that rush and days that drag.

Deliver me from the ache of friends gone,
from endless mourning and confined vision.
> May I pass through consuming darkness
> that fails to see a dawn.

Falcon-like, lift me up
above the breaking waves.
> Let me glimpse beyond stages of mourning.
> Set me down in a velvet valley.

May I be transformed
by gatherings and greetings,
> succored from life's half-filled glass
> and from encounters with creatures of other kinds.

Soothe me with greenery and solitude.
May I find a transit point, a Golden Gate,
> even though I pass snaillike through grief.
> Awaken my spirit to signals of transcendence.

Image: The scene at Point Reyes, with the snail, the falcon, the deer, the whale. Savor their vibrancy. Bring to mind a good memory of those missed or mourned. Pray for their spring transit point.

You might also pray for some area within your own life that needs to seek a transit point.

Journal: I need to pass beyond...

Praying with the Salmon

The salmon, with its amazing heroic quest that challenges the limits of its endurance, is a creature extolled in imagery and myth. In ancient Celtic mythology, the hero's perilous passage is called "the salmon's leap." Later in Irish Christian parlance, the act of religious faith is also sometimes referred to in those terms. Celtic myth considers the salmon as the oldest and most knowing creature.

> ...the Celtic "Salmon of Knowledge" gains wisdom while swimming in the sacred pool amid the nine trees of knowledge.... Whoever would catch a Salmon of Knowledge would be flooded with inspiration by one taste of it.[2]

Ancient people in northern Japan believed that the salmon were returning spirits who were sacrificing themselves and thus ensuring future life.

The Salmon's Heroic Quest

In an ice-cold stream far inland, young salmon hatch in the fresh water and, as they develop, begin to swim and feed. This particular spot where they hatch, with its own rocks, trees and green shore, will be their own. It is the transit point of their origin and their returning destiny. For the salmon, this place is like no other, and the salmon shall never forget.

As the fish grow, a deep instinct begins to lure them toward the faraway sea, and each salmon begins a momentous journey downstream. The agile fish makes some of this journey with ease. It is a swift journey, but not without peril. Along the way, it must cope with many obstacles, not the least being environmental havoc wreaked by the human species.

If it survives, the salmon reaches the ocean. Free at last! In the sea, it feeds and grows. It still must beware of drift nets and predators. After sometimes traveling thousands of miles at sea, the voyager begins an epic journey back to its point of origin. That is the only place it will spawn.

The map for this journey is coded into the deepest instinct of the salmon. How marvelous it would be if we could eat of the "Salmon of Knowledge," if we could decode the inner circuitry. What if the push to the sea and the painstaking pull back to its fresh water origin could be translated into human words? What a hero's story it would tell!

Or if by some magic we could shrink in size and swim with the salmon, sharing its agility and destiny, and record a journal of the journey—if we could, it might read like this:

JOURNALING WITH THE SALMON

The sights we have seen! Whales and sharks, friendly neighbors and deadly predators, submarines, the hulls of tankers and twirling propellers! We are the survivors. We have avoided the drift nets, the worst obstacle of all. These greedy death traps can stretch for miles to a depth of thirty feet. We escaped by being in the right place at the right time. Not so for thousands of our comrades....

We have been gone from home for a year now and we are now fat and sassy—salt water sailors. Sometimes I wonder why we can't just stay right here and enjoy all this good eating for many years to come....

Today, we are far out into the Pacific, facing westward, but this morning, we reached our farthest point. We hesitate. We feel a tension. The sea is drawing us, but there is something else pulling us back, something very deep within the being of every salmon.

The pull is eastward. We all sense that somehow, some way, we must return....

We shall go back together. This afternoon, we turn. Our course is now landward. We shall not be dissuaded.

Our course is now set. It will be many days before we reach shore, for we have traveled thousands of miles in our journey since leaving home. We are strong and we are determined. We shall return....

Today, the water grows more shallow. We are being pulled by the tide. Land is not far off.

Like stealth planes coming in under radar, we hone in under the tide. There are hundreds of rivers that run down to the sea. We seek only one. It is our own. We shall know it. We shall rendezvous....

Today, land is in sight. Soon—the navigation from salt water to fresh. Then there will be more formidable obstacles. We must feed up for the remaining journey....

Our number dissipates. The journey is more lonely. Of the three thousand eggs laid by one mother, only a handful from that hatch have made it this far in the journey....

We are landlocked, moving up a fresh water stream now. We are banged against rocks and buffeted on every side. We are slowed down—but not deterred....

It seems as though there are lookouts all along the shore. The trees do not harm us, but there are fishermen and fisher animals. This is a narrowing escape path. We are fugitives on a most-wanted list....

More and more energy is needed. Deep resources of strength must be mustered in order to leap up out of the water and beyond. A moment ago a dam loomed up straight ahead. After many leaps to no avail, a man-made passageway is discovered. It is so strange: Humans are the enemy, yet they do provide for some salmon to escape. Some of them must want this species to survive. We angle through the narrow way and leap up over and over and over again....

The constant struggle to fight our way upstream has brought great weariness. Aging is accelerated. The river journey has been like the transit from midlife to the ranks of the elderly. It is difficult to press on....

Today, we survivors are in the wilds beyond human pursuit. This morning a huge shadow appeared over the stream. A large paw swiped down and snatched the fish next to me right out of the water. For an instant it was eyeball to eyeball with a hungry bear. Like a juggler he tried to get hold of the wriggling salmon. At the last instant it slipped from his grasp and lunged back into the stream....

We have moved beyond many dangers. There are so few of us left now. I observe the remnant. We are slowing down. We begin to circle. We sense being at home. This is our place, our point of origin. The deepest core of our being has brought us home. The genetic map passed down through eons has brought us back to the very place where we were hatched. Now is it is our turn to spawn and then to die. The compass has been true. We need go no farther....

We summon our last energies. The eggs are placed on the stream's floor. The circle is complete. Energy is spent. It is done. Drawn towards the shore, all around me silver and crimson bodies begin to float sideways. There is a letting go. New life will come. Destiny is fulfilled. The epic journey has been fulfilled.

Prayer of the Salmon Journey

Holy One, Sacred End of all longing,
  may the epic journey of the courageous salmon
  inspire me on my way to you.

At the times when I move **downstream**,
  passing along swift channels, going with the flow,
  things going my way,
  traversing the turns with ease of motion,
  may my prayer leap up in *Thanks! Thanks! Thanks!*

When I pass into the **wider currents**,
  and I can float on the surface of life,
  and all seems well and calm,
  may I be delivered from the subtle danger
  of drifting into hidden nets beneath placid waters.

When I move down **into the depths**,
  guide me through murky waters and over sunken hulks.
  Let visions and images swirl in the deep places.
  May I surface my dream guided by my inner vision.

As I reach a **transit point**,
  knowing that my journey
  cannot avoid monsters of the deep,
  may I discern the transit point, get to the point
  and make my way through inky black waters.

As I make my **move upstream**,
  help me to see that every turning point
  is a time for courageous leaps,
  up, out, above seeking sight.
  May I move against the flow and clamor to conform.

May I make the *leap beyond*
  the bear paws of shutdowns, rejections and addictions.
  Preserve me from financial despair caused by bear markets.
  Let me navigate with poise and skill one day at a time.

When I must traverse *the narrow way*, *the tight channel*,
  the needle's eye that demands courage,
  prayer, and even fasting,
  may I squeeze through whatever tightens life:
  difficult decisions, depressions, deaths
  and losses small and great.

Bring me *home again*,
  having paid the bruising price of the narrow way.
  May I maintain my faith and trust
  in origins and a gracious destiny.
  Bring me home again and again
  through spring's transformations.

Image: The segment of the salmon's journey that is most like yours right now. Pray for the grace, skill and agility you will need to pass this transit point...

Journal: On my journey, I...

PRAYING WITH THE WILD GEESE

Moving in broad fronts, an estimated 5 billion birds migrate between watering areas as far south as Tierra del Fuego, Argentina, and nesting grounds as far north as Point Barrow, Alaska. On any given night, spring or fall, hundreds of millions of migrant birds are flying over the commercial United States and its offshore waters.

Jack Connor, *Nature Conservancy*,
November/December 1995

Rudyard Kipling chose the image of the wild geese to describe the heroic adventures of the wild Gaels of Ireland. It was a worthy choice, for a formation of wild geese, their long necks stretched "head to the storm," form an undaunted column. They brave turbulence undeterred on their transcontinental journeys.

With their noble bearing, it is no wonder geese are revered in many cultures. The Indian deity Brahma, for example, is pictured riding on the back of one of these graceful birds. In ancient Rome, geese were honored for having warned the citizens of the capital about the approach of the marauding Gauls.

The snails crawl; the salmon leap; the wild geese fly in squadrons beyond confinement. When the first faint sounds of the geese drift down from spring's skies like the echoes of muffled trumpets, they announce a passage through the curtain of winter's long night. They herald a passover beyond the limits of our horizon.

They call us to look up and look out. Their passage is spring's alarm clock. The honking geese shake us from winter's sleep and alert us to peer out at our global home and to take flight with our imaginations toward what might lie beyond.

Migration—Life's Push and Pull

Their journey's course is imprinted on some ancient interior map. They are pushed by the mysterious migratory instinct. But more than that, they seem pulled by an allurement that permeates our planet. Some final cause draws them toward their hearts' yearnings.

Their spring transit might stir within us our heart's quest. Is there not within us a pull, a yearning to vault beyond the restraints, beyond the petty barricades of daily strife? Do we not sense an allurement to fly beyond our last lurking limitation, the confines of death?

Beyond Limitations

The DNA of such diverse creatures as the salmon and the geese empowers them to make their amazing journeys in spite of enormously adverse odds. For the human species, the greatest obstacle in the way of our life-quest is death itself. Yet in the human evolutionary journey the imagination of homo sapiens possesses the unique ability to dream—to imagine and then to move beyond seemingly insurmountable limitations. We have moved from walking to flying, from earth travel to space travel, and only the human has dared to dream of life beyond death. Such a dream is either a foolish illusion or a wondrous potential development, its power to be imagined planted in our DNA. Is it not possible that the divine energy which pulls the salmon and geese to their destiny can also pull humans toward transcendent hope and dreams?

The leaping salmon and the V formations of migrating geese writing their message in the sky can give us pause to wonder—and to dream once more of what lies beyond our own horizons.

V

Each spring and fall in North America, the glorious geese spread across the skies in their symmetrical V formations. Their sounds descend from the heavens, heralding the change of seasons. Before the advent of airplanes, other than the crashing thunder, they were among the few messengers to speak to us from high in the clouds.

Flyways

Geese are among one hundred million waterfowl that fly north and south across four North American flyways. Some of their ancestors have sailed along these routes for more than a million years. Some fly as much as seven thousand miles between Canada and South America. Without radio or radar, they unerringly find their way across these vast distances.

After the usually harsh winters of the northern plains, the sound of geese in the night sky is like a polyphonic choir announcing the breaking of winter's icy grip. Fields and fountains will soon be released from icy bondage. The whitened sandhills will be transformed to green. The spring crossing of the geese is like a blessing prayer over spring's transformation.

A Vibrant Fountain

At De Soto Refuge near Blair, Nebraska, over five hundred thousand geese pass through during a migrating season. At any one time, there might be one hundred and seventy thousand birds pausing to rest and feed there. When thousands of these geese rise up out of the waters at one time, it is like a white cascading fountain that splashes against the blue sky.

Out of an explosion of flailing wings, the formations emerge. Millennia before Dwight Eisenhower flashed the familiar "V for victory" sign, the forebears of these geese have written their "V" large across the sky. Their sign might remind us of valiant spring journeys that lift the human spirit from icy confinement.

North - South

The north-south trajectory of the migrating birds might also remind us that all creatures share one globe—north, south, east and west. The journey of the geese down, rather than across, counters our human preoccupation with east and west. On a global scale, North Americans have tended to be people who look only east and west—a narrow view. Human transcontinental migrations were east to west, and the long cold war focused our attention on Russia to the east and Vietnam to the west.

Perhaps we have forgotten what Native Americans have known so well: that all directions are holy. The geese, cranes and other migratory birds crisscross our human paths and thoroughfares. They know no borders. They violate no illegal boundaries. They are not aliens because for them planet earth is home. They value the frozen north as well as the sunny south. Their clarion call, north to south, might well remind us of our need for a more wholistic, global view.

PRAYER OF THE GEESE'S FLIGHT

Wild   geese

   sweeping above   our night dreams

     arch over   winter shadows

      Hark! The heralds   of spring

        valiant   squadrons

         heads to   the storm

          spring's   vanguards

           victor's   flight

"V"

Spirit of the heights and the depths,
who allures our human striving,
this day and every day
help me to fly.

Like the high-flying wild geese,
attracted beyond their horizon,
may I be caught up in the divine allurement
that pulls me toward fulfillment.
Like the wild geese, who stick their necks out,
may I surge ahead,
flying above the downdrafts of lost opportunities
and the turbulence of disappointments.

Like the wild geese, who break a path for each other,
may I find companions for the journey,
who form the symmetry of communal care, of friendship,
not holding me back or keeping me in line but helping me on.

Like the wild geese, who know when to take flight,
may I know the time of my seasons,
sensitive to each proper passageway,
the springtime of each day's new beginning.

Like the wild geese, who take turns at the point of the "V,"
may I be willing to take my turn,
being wise enough to know when to follow and to learn,
and ready at the right moment to lead and move ahead.

Like the wild geese, who surmount incredible obstacles,
spurred on by unfailing inner resolve,
may I find the courage to pass over transit points
coaxed on by my deepest allurements.

Like two wild geese falling out
to companion a wounded fellow,

may I console and be consoled, nurture and be nurtured,
rather than rescue or be rescued.

Like the wild geese passing through a storm,
may I fly from denial
toward awareness
and a willingness to change course to reach my goals.
Like the wild geese, who write "V" in the sky,
not in triumph over creatures,
but as a signal of spring,
may I break out of icy, rigid bonds that confine my spirit.

Like the wild geese, who rise up through chaotic flutter,
may I ascend from chaos
and wind my way through messiness
to find the flight path and direction for my journey.

Like the wild geese, who traverse the wide world
may I scan the vast horizon
—east, west, north and south—
and glimpse the wide and wonderful world all around me.

Transforming Spirit,
each morning in the course of my life flight
may I rise up from inertia into the graceful "V"
that signals movement and meaningful direction.

Image: The "V" flight of the geese. Identify one of the prayer paragraphs above that you especially need to pray today or tomorrow and expand upon it in your continuing prayer.

Journal: Like the geese, I...

Chapter Three

Praying with the Saguaro Cactus,
Eagle
and Desert Tortoise

PRAYERS FOR DESERT TIMES

Several years ago, as I drove north from Phoenix, up through the Valley of the Sun, I was struck by a prayerful presence—the Saguaro cacti towering beside the road. Their arms reached up as if in prayer. Like beggars awaiting a treasured pittance, their posture seemed to proclaim, "Even as we wait for the rare and precious gift of rain, we are grateful for the sun."

I journeyed through this cactus valley on my way to the desert rim and beyond to Payson in the piney woods. There I would experience a weekend retreat, seek a vision and endure the heat of a Native American sweat lodge.

Like the Saguaro, I was seeking living water for my inner depths. The desert times of our lives can lead us to such a search. Sometimes, it seems we must journey through a wasteland before any oasis can appear. Like the Hebrew people, we too often encounter the fierceness of desert testing before entering a land of promise.

In such desert journeys, we might be taught by those who have survived in the badlands. In our own southwest, survivors like the saguaro, the desert tortoise, and the Native American peoples possess a wisdom fired in the furnace of desert living.

At a secluded retreat I joined a most ecumenical group. Our leader was Carl, a psychiatrist and author. Early on in his medical practice, Carl was attracted to the healing ways of the Native American medicine men and women, finding a wisdom there not to be gleaned from medical books. Subsequently he founded a learning and growth-oriented movement, the Turtle Island Project. Our weekend was to be a segment of that project. Our group included Lutherans, Jews, Catholics and a Mormon among others.

We were to be led in our sweat lodge by a Native American medicine woman.

Our sweat lodge day began before dawn with each of us embarking on an abridged vision quest. We spent time alone in the midst of nature, seeking a vision, perhaps of a creature that would speak to the depths of our imaginations. The theme of this book is based precisely on the belief that the creatures who cohabit this earth with us have something to teach us that springs from their unique evolutionary development. Their lineage comes down from the elders of prehuman history. We avoid their ancient wisdom to our peril. When open, we are immeasurably enriched.

At dawn, we entered the sweat lodge. Thirty-two rocks had been preheated. They were glowing red in the misty dawn. That sweat lodge was a deep and rich experience. Yet no depth experience can be described adequately in words. It can only be slightly approximated through images. In some sense, in the sweat lodge, I felt something about what the cactus feels from the searing summer heat and the black canopy of the desert night.

Four times over several hours the medicine woman brought more red-hot rocks into the tiny pitch-black enclosure. When she splashed them with water, steam invaded every pore. It was so pervasive that it seemed to pass right through the body, sucking vitality from every cell.

And in the dark, we prayed to the Spirit, each in his or her own fashion. It seemed for me that I was cast back into my childhood, and long-forgotten ancient Latin and Greek prayers escaped from somewhere very deep within me: "*Asperges me, Domine, hyssopo*! Sprinkle me, O Lord, with hyssop, and I shall be purified; wash me, and I shall be whiter than snow!...*Kyrie Eleison*! *Kyrie Eleison*! Lord have mercy! Lord have mercy!" My chant mixed with Hebrew and Native American cries. Something very primeval had been loosened up in all of us, and it streamed out of our psyches while the sweat poured from our bodies.

When we left the lodge, Carl knelt and reverently kissed the earth. We had been somewhere else, and now we had returned to earth.

Our sweat-lodge journey had consumed the morning; after a light lunch I began the journey down from the mountains and through the desert saguaro country. As I passed the saguaros, I had a deeper appreciation and empathy for their endurance. I traveled in an open jeep, and the heat again was intense. The highway shimmered and danced in the fierce Arizona sun. I had been up since before dawn, and a concern began to nag me. At 6:30 that evening, I was to address three hundred people. I wondered if I would have an ounce of energy left after this cathartic and draining day.

I arrived shortly before the talk with no opportunity to rest. When I arose to give my address, something very amazing occurred. I felt more energized than for any talk I had given that year! I was alert and my whole message seemed to emerge from a hidden wellspring of untapped energy.

What was that all about? I was puzzled. Was I flying high on adrenaline? Or could it be that the desert so strips us that we must travel light and rely on our deepest resources? Did the sweat-lodge experience enforce that removal of the excess baggage, allowing the deepest spirit to emerge?

I think a saguaro would probably know the answer.

Praying with the Saguaro

The saguaro is the old wise one of the wastelands. This barrel-chested cactus made famous in many western movies endures the sweat lodge of the desert and thrives in the worst of times. This giant of the Sonoran desert regions possesses great wisdom for the desert times of our lives.

The saguaro is a survivor. At first it hovers below the shade of a nurse plant. It waits and waits for the opportune time to seize the moment and emerge on its own. It develops for fifty or sixty years before it is ready to bring forth its first flower. At just the right time, usually in the month of May, it bursts into bloom, but each blossom lives for only twenty-four hours. Over a lifetime, which can span as many as two hundred years, it produces as many as twenty-two million seeds. Out of this abundance perhaps only one seed will survive to germinate and reproduce!

This desert giant stores within itself living water. It also develops its own prickly "beard," which not only discourages hostile predators but also serves as its own air-conditioning system —so essential in a parched land where daytime temperatures soar over the hundred degree mark for months on end.

In its infancy, the tiny cactus depends upon the shade of a nurse plant of another species while it gradually stores up an inner reservoir of life-giving water. The protecting nurse plant also offers some shelter from potential molesters. When the cactus reaches adulthood, it too becomes generous and hospitable. Birds hollow out cavities and nest within it. Its desert wisdom proclaims endurance, adaptation and hospitality in one of the most inhospitable of any climates.

The Holy Home of the Saguaro

The saguaro, arms uplifted as though in prayer, might remind us that for countless ages its desert home has been viewed by spiritual seekers as a special prayer space. In the long history of prayer, the desert has often been seen as a holy locale where seekers can travel light and encounter spiritual realities. The desert, whether of sand or of our inner souls, challenges us to see more clearly and to travel with prayer as our best companion.

Praying for the Blessings of the Saguaro

Creator of all life and resiliency,
sometimes the global turmoil of every newscast
and the grind of my own daily struggles
sear and parch my soul.

Why don't they make things better?
Perhaps I long for nurse plants
to shelter me,
rescue me, nourish me?

Most of my daily images assure me:
of a quick fix—guzzle it;
move it; leave it;
it's better over there.

But the saguaro teaches me
that often the blessings I seek
are really deep down
within my spirit!

Great prickly giants,
like Moses, arms extended,
holding your ground,
bless my thirst.

May your wise and merciful creator
replenish the desert seasons of my life,
the arroyos of eroded dreams,
the parched seasons of discontent.
May I have your saguaro's inner strength to
Wait
Hold
Stay
Endure

May I learn that beneath barbed defenses
and below our hollow wounds
flows the wellspring of our deepest being,
living water
that will see us through.

I pray that this desert period of my life
will prove to be a holy time to stay still,
an opportune moment to lay low,
as I wait for a better day
for breaking camp and making tracks.

May I enter the spirituality of the desert,
and obtain the blessings of the saguaro:
endurance,
adaptation,
hospitality.

Image: The saguaro standing tall and green, surrounded by the desert's sun-baked sand. Call to mind stored-up memories of times when you were in dire-dry straits. Remember how you survived and trust you shall do so again. Renew your hope in prayer.

Journal: The deepest water within me...

Praying with the Eagle

A Golden Eagle was discovered in Ireland, bedraggled and emaciated. It was so weak that it could be picked up off the ground. Its presence was a mystery, for there are no golden eagles in Ireland. Its journey had been trans-oceanic. After deliberating about exhibiting this unusual bird in a zoo, an ancient celtic kinship with the animal world prevailed. The eagle was placed on an *Aer Lingus* jet liner, returned to the United States, and released in the wilds.

Eddie Burke, Irish storyteller, Kilkenny

The lofty eagle surveys the edge of the desert rim with a majestic stare. High up in the thermals, almost suspended, she is the prototype of the observer plane. She can also dive down upon her prey with pinpoint accuracy.

The golden eagle, the most common eagle in North America, sometimes "goes steady" with her future mate from age two till sexual maturity at five, and then bonds for life. During courting, she can perform an amazing aerial display in which she quickly turns upside down in mid-flight as her suitor nose-dives and touches her claw.

If the saguaro is the sentinel of the desert valley, the eagle is the messenger from the craggy heights that summons us up from the valleys of our discontent. Whether for couples in love, or couples on rocky ground, or single parents, the eagle's exuberance and devotion to its nest is an uplifting symbol of endurance.

When we are mired in the desert of daily drudgery, at work or at home, the free-flying eagle can give us a glimpse of new possibilities. For those who are downtrodden, depressed or even verging on despair, the eagle's flight can be a reminder of our capacity for a wider vision.

To Native Americans, the eagle is a sacred bird. The eagle feather is used in sacred ceremonies. At Whiteriver on the Apache reservation, the Franciscan Friars have been given permission to use the sacred eagle feather when incense is used in church ceremonies. In this sacred smudging, the feather wafts the swirling incense around the worshiper in a rite of purification.

Carl, the psychiatrist who invited us to the vision quest and sweat lodge, has a weekly "talking circle" in his office. Anyone may come. The eagle feather is passed, and the one holding it speaks a truth that emerges from deep within. The speakers can share anything on their minds or in their hearts. There is no response or critique from the others, just a reverential listening. In such a sacred circle, the eagle feather can begin to summon participants out of the valleys of discontent towards a higher wisdom.

The eagle flies over forests, deserts, valleys and plains, but it always seeks a higher place. When the bald eagle soars over the flatlands of Nebraska, it flies to the high branches of the cottonwoods on the banks of the Missouri River. There in the wintertime, its silhouette high in the branches defies any storm to bring it down.

If we were to think of the eagle as a totem unique to the Native Americans, we would miss the mark. Almost all Americans carry with them an image of the eagle. Emblazoned on the U.S. dollar bill, the eagle clasps both the olive branch of peace as well as the arrows of war. Its image conveys strength and determination. We too are endowed with the capacity to deal with conflict, to soar beyond petty concerns and disagreements and seek higher ground.

The eagle reminds us of our own inner strength and higher wisdom. If our life journey stumbles upon scorched and barren ground, the eagle's quest can rouse our imagination from torpor.

The Vision Questing Prayer of the Eagle

These desert days I am earthbound,
my vision obscured by glare,
my own path rutted and fissured,
my prayer like ashes in my mouth.

These are the worst of unrelenting days
and restless, dreamless nights.
My scorched path slows my plodding.
I fail to look up and beyond.

Earthbound, I sense only where I have been,
and where I am now,
not how much more there is to see,
nor where I might hope to be.

Divine Spirit, far beyond the vault of the heavens
yet as close as my heart's nest,
may I soar unto the eagle skyway
to look wider, view farther.

I pray for an ascending spirit,
a share in winged courage,
an eagle's eye discerning
a better way to go.

Image: The eagle soaring. See its view from the heights. Pray for perspective, discernment, for an unfolding vision.

Journal: On eagle's wings I shall...

PRAYING WITH THE DESERT TORTOISE

According to Native American legend, the earth is supported on the back of a giant turtle. The turtle's slow, deliberate movement provides for changes of time and seasons. An impenetrable fortress, when threatened, it finds strength within. But it makes progress only when it sticks out its neck. The ancients called this whole world "Turtle Island."

Carl Hammerslaug, pamphlet from
The Turtle Island Project

Out in the hostile terrain of the desert, victory comes to survivors such as the desert tortoise. Like a grizzled and veteran infantryman, the tortoise wears its own camouflaged helmet and sticks its neck out only with great care. Shielded from the eagle's dive, and lost in the dust of swifter creatures, the sleepy-eyed tortoise plods along with minimum speed and maximum determination toward its cool, safe hole in the desert sand.

Back in the human fast lane, our myths proclaim that victory comes to the swift competitor. So we scramble to beat our endless deadlines. Yellow lights mean "Hurry up," not "Slow down." We rush through life like roadrunners. We work harder and longer than ever before so we can buy more gadgets that we don't find time to use. We expend our energies in great, furious bursts. And sometimes, we burn out like fizzled rockets in the sky, dropping back to earth exhausted, deflated, impoverished.

If we land in the desert, we might meet the tortoise, who has been around for hundreds of millions of years and who knows something about winning. If we could only sit at his feet for awhile and dialogue. Yet perhaps we can in the fertile ground of our imaginations:

"Mister Turtle, what on earth are you doing here? I thought creatures like you lived in the ocean?"

"Oh, a long time ago that was true. But some of us were landlocked when the great waters receded, and so we became desert tortoises. We made the best of what we had."

"How can you make the best of such a barren place?"

"By living carefully and unhurriedly."

"But where will that get you?"

"Well, every time we race the hare, we come out ahead in the long run. No race is won in a day. Life is a marathon."

"I don't know about that. For me it's been a rat race. Every day I'm surrounded by cheap-shot artists, and lately I've taken a few too many hits."

"Don't you have a shell? I just pull my head in under my shell and stay calm for awhile. The coyotes sniff, but after awhile they howl somewhere else.

"It can storm outside, but I let the furies blow around me. Inside my shell I have a safe house. Don't you have a calm inner center?"

"Not exactly; mine is filled with Maalox."

"Maybe you should tune into our song: 'Slow down, you move too fast; you've got to make the moment last!'

"When the dinosaurs came around ranting and raving, our ancestors played our song, not theirs. They were the 'corporate giants' of their day. They strode over valleys and toppled boulders. My folks traveled about twenty feet per minute. We're still moving. Haven't seen any dinosaur lately though."

PRAYER OF THE TORTOISE

Creator God,
whose impulse underlies the tiniest movement,
be my companion and guide
as I make my way
home to you.

Deserted in the desert,
turned over and exposed,
I renew my faith in unexpected favors,
grace-filled turnabouts,
last minute comebacks.

As I cast my own long shadow
in the sinking desert sun,
may I not be overcome by shadowy memories,
by dinosaurs of my own imagining,
by ancient scars.

Let the predators of life's rat race,
the tarantulas and leaping lizards,
the roadrunners and coyotes,
go their way,
while I go mine.

O God, accompanied by your silent presence,
one step at a time, day by day,
with unmeasured pace,
steadied by my calm inner center,
I shall pass over and be free.

Image: The desert tortoise sitting in the shade of the saguaro. He nods his head at you. What does this image have to say to your life these days? Pray about that message.

Journal: As I make my way through the desert...

Chapter Four

Praying with the Grizzly Bear,
Polar Bear
and Wolf

Prayers for Hard Frozen Times

Praying with the Grizzly Bear

Lessons for humans from the Grizzly Bear: stability, durability, healing, introspection, awareness, maturity, leadership and teaching.

Sun Bear, Wabun, and Crysalis Mulligan,
Dancing with the Wheel

She runs with amazing agility, her brown fur rippling like a waving field of grain. She is the grizzly, the most magnificent four-legged creature of the North American forests. For the Native Americans she stands for good medicine. For her cubs, she is a tender and playful mother. For the stock market, she is an omen of trouble.

For a friend of mine on a memorable afternoon in Alaska, she became a teacher of awareness and of human limitations.

Jack had worked in Montana for the Forest Service for most of his life. Over this lifetime he had encountered almost every wild creature native to the Big Sky country. Only in his peaceful first year of retirement, however, would he come face to face with the biggest and most powerful creature of them all.

It happened at an unlikely time—broad daylight, in a mountain wilderness. Having packed only his camera, he was walking along an ill-defined trail that wound parallel to a ridge line. To his right stretched an alpine meadow extending up the side of the nearest mountain. He was far removed from any trees. He was highly visible. He was alone, he thought.

He walked in the clear splendor of a sun-filled day, yet there were shadows. There always are on the best of days. As he made his way, a foreboding began to creep along the edges of his consciousness. There was an uneasy silence. No birds, no sounds, as though all the creatures of meadow and forest had stepped back and out of the way, not in deference to his coming, but rather in obeisance to the arrival of some sovereign in the shadowy woods.

Jack paused. His eyes scanned the meadow. Nothing. Then, he peered at the forest edge—only dark shadows. "Shadows!" he thought. "Am I being shadowed?" The hair on his neck bristled, for out of the corner of his eye he detected movement. In the next moment, out of the shadows came a rustling of fur and a flash of eyes. From the tree line, a gigantic grizzly was staring directly at him. It was as though a powerful diesel railroad engine had emerged suddenly from a tunnel with its intense headlight beaming directly upon him.

Jack realized immediately that his own presence was highly visible and very vulnerable. He was in more danger than if he were standing on a track with a train bearing down on him. You might leap out of the way of a locomotive, but with the bear's agility and speed there was no way to sidestep, no place to hide and no sense in trying to run away.

Gulping down a feeling of panic, Jack decided to move slowly ahead, hoping against hope that his own nonthreatening movements would cause the bear to lose interest. However, as he cautiously moved forward on a course parallel to the bear's, out of his right eye he could see the bear closing distance. Each step Jack took forward, the grizzly took one forward and downward in his direction. He was on a collision course with jaws of death.

At that point, he had only one strategy left. He described it this way: "I stopped dead in my tracks. I became very still and very humble. Sometimes you need to move quickly, but there are other times when all you can do is stop and wait. I avoided any eye contact and any movement. I assumed a totally submissive pose. I bowed my head in prayer and in fright. I could sense the movements of the bear through the meadow grass. It got closer. I held my pose of submission and utter quiet. After a minute collapsed into an eternity, I heard nothing. When I dared to look up, she was on the horizon and moving beyond me. She had lost interest."

There are hard times in our lives when all we can do is stop, freeze in our tracks, and wait with intense awareness. In those moments, we become aware that we are not in control, yet our letting go can mean deliverance.

Jack's story is a true one. There is another apocryphal bear story about a priest, rabbi and minister camping in Alaska in the fall. The first night at camp an early snow fell. In the morning, there seemed to be bear tracks around the edge of camp. The rabbi noticed them and alerted the minister. They talked about the tracks, and each decided to choose a tree to climb in case the bear would show up. When they alerted the Catholic priest, he responded, "I haven't noticed any bear tracks. Why bother with a tree to climb?"

That night, at midnight, a crashing sound was heard in the underbrush. The priest's two friends bounded out of their tents and climbed their nearest trees. The priest stuck his head out of his tent and laughed at them, "That's not a bear sound! The bears are hibernating now!"

A few moments later, a large bear emerged and peered into the priest's tent. A little embarrassed, the priest exclaimed, "Well I was wrong about there not being a bear, but he looks harmless."

Then the bear knelt down by the campfire and folded his paws together as if in prayer. "Look at this!" cried the priest. "This is not only a safe bear but a pious one. It looks like its going to pray!" Then the bear did an amazing thing. With one paw it made the sign of the cross! Now the priest roared with laughter. "Ha! This is not only a pious bear, but it's also a Catholic bear!

I've nothing to fear."

The bear then folded its paws and growled its own prayer: "Bless me, O Lord, for this meal which I am about to receive."

GOOD MEDICINE

Laughter is good medicine. So are bears for the Native Americans. When a nosy bear flushes out bees instead of honey, the scene can be comical, all the more so because the normal persona of the bear is majestic and commanding.

There is a right time for laughter and warmth. There is also a time to freeze in our tracks, as Jack did when he encountered the grizzly. Grizzlies can symbolize forces of nature and life that are awesome and intimidating. An encounter with a grizzly would make anyone's heart skip with dread. So can other hard life experiences. Yet perhaps such a heart's skip may provide just the pause we need to awaken within ourselves our own bear-like inner reserves of great-heartedness. At such vulnerable moments in our lives, becoming very still and silent can be like a mini-hibernation, a pause that allows inner dynamisms and untapped reserves to be marshaled.

Other life experiences may demand swift movement. Bears are symbols of good medicine for us because they know the right time and the right place. They know when to hibernate, when to awake, when to seek the salmon and caribou. They are adept at adjusting to their terrain. Many of them can climb a tree. All know how to saunter through a dense forest, sprint across a meadow, fish at a stream and sniff the prevailing winds.

When we experience the winter hardships of our human spirits, we need remedies. The bear experience and the bear symbolism offers us a medicine chest filled with good medicine.

URSUS HORRIBILIS!

The grizzly (*ursus horribilis*) is the most powerful creature in North America. Fiercely independent, it fends for itself and is thus seen as the wise one of the forest.

Had the grizzly that tracked Jack actually closed in on him, he would have faced nine hundred pounds of raw power. He would have looked up into the face of an eight-foot giant with one-and-a-half inch teeth capable of piercing anything from a man to a moose.

BEAR SYMBOLISM

The tortoise's shelled defense in the desert symbolizes the life moments when we would best hold our ground, or even play possum as Jack did before the grizzly. However, there are other hard times when we would best make our move. Bear energy is about movement, agility and awakened power.

Roused from introspection, the bear awakens, emerges and acts decisively. An aroused grizzly charging across a meadow is a blur of fur and paws capable of attaining speeds up to 30 miles per hour.

Bears dream long winter dreams, but when the time comes to arise, to move, to seek their path, they know the way to go.

Prayer of the Bear Within Me

On my daily trail—
when my path takes the wrong turn,
when I am exposed and stressed,
when there seems no place to run toward,
and no place to hide—
let me pause, sniff the wind,
hunker down and gather strength,
summoning up my own inner bear wisdom.

Let my own bear energy
growl, snort and roar!
I am not a flower to be trampled,
nor a co-dependent sapling to be wasted.
Standing tall like the grizzly,
seeing beyond denial or threats,
I have the moxie
to know the forest from the trees.

Great Spirit, dynamic source of bear energy,
stir up my bear spirit.
Summon me from the cave of my dreams.
This day I must stretch, snarl, open my eyes.
I can see the daylight beckoning.
Let me prowl through hostile territory.
Pawing my way through thickets,
I have "nothing to fear but fear itself."

Image: The mighty grizzly, standing straight up, peering ahead.

Journal: My own bear wisdom and deep energy summon me...

POLAR BEAR TRACKS

For many species, migrations provide dramatic changes of scene and temperature. Not for the polar bears. These lumbering giants gut their way through ice and storm and maintain their white overcoats through all seasons. The tougher the sledding the greater the challenge for these arctic travellers.

In contrast to desert creatures who hunker down in the sweltering heat, the polar bear exemplifies determination and mobility, sometimes traveling six or seven hundred miles over icy waters to find a food source.

Despite their great bulk, the polar bears' movements can be agile and swift, whether loping over snow fields or swimming through icy waters. In a climate that makes fierce demands on bodily resources, they are able to focus their energies to achieve maximum effects. They possess a finely honed instinctual wisdom that tells them when to slumber and when to sprint. Like fighter planes resting beneath a mother ship and refueling in flight, these bears can lumber along in a semi-hibernating trance and then come to full alert and shift to maximum throttle. They make bold tracks across the ice fields and fear no other creature, including man.

Our Ice Fields

As a human species we encounter our own ice fields. Sometimes we take hard falls on the icy paths of daily life, or experience the coldness of alienation. We suffer from relationships which turn frigid, from blocked advancements, from the aging and cooling of passion, from bear markets and frozen rejections. Sometimes cold water is thrown upon our dreams and plans. Stress, like subzero temperatures, can contract and constrict our spirits.

Our addictions and obsessions can be like creeping glaciers that day by day gouge out a bit more of our soul. Encapsuled in their icy grip, we deny their power. The poet Dante in his epic *The Divine Comedy* traced the journey of the soul and described the descent into hell as a descent into ice!

Ten percent of our globe is encased in glacial ice! We might ask how much of our own life is ice-laden, frozen by behaviors that need to melt and become life-giving streams. That is what recovery groups are about—melting the ice that contracts and setting loose the energy that warms our hearts and expands our spirits.

When our path is snowy and our spirits frozen, shall we read the bear tracks and become alert to the signs of the times? Shall we let our bear experiences teach us, or will they simply devour us?

PRAYER FOR GOOD BEAR MEDICINE

Great Spirit,
grant me bear wisdom and courage,
the good medicine of standing tall
like a grizzly,
tracking through storms
like the polar,
introspecting and hibernating
like the black bear.

When I am the white bear of the north,
out in the cold from plunging bear markets,
freeze-outs and burnouts,
arctic chills and unpaid bills,
iced friends and frozen dreams;
when I feel stranded out on the tundra,
surrounded by drifted cares
and black-iced hopes,
stalked by the gales of despair,
let me sniff the wind,
sense my strength,
make the right tracks.

When I am the prey,
of sharp tooth competitors,
of growling bosses or pawing co-workers,
of relentless climbers,
of nosy, sniffing neighbors,
of devouring cynics or fanged critics—
may I be girded with survival skills.
Let me find the snow shelter,
the quiet center point
in the eye in the storm,
for these gales shall pass,
this blizzard shall abate.

When I am black bear of the south,
> tired from bustling through the brambles,
> making my way relentlessly in the fading sun,
>> may I change the seasons,
>> hibernate, luxuriate, commiserate,
> like the good medicine bear
> dear to Native Americans.
>> Perhaps I can be a teddy bear,
>> or a roly-poly panda
>> or an enchanting koala.
> Where's Goldylocks?
> Afraid of being mugged?
>> I'll give bear hugs.
>> In the giving I'll find the honey.

Image: The polar bear on the ice-fields—or the teddy bear of your childhood. Pray your own polar bear prayer or teddy bear prayer for this cold period in your journey.

Journal: On my hard, frozen life-path, the insight and good medicine I receive from the bear...

Praying with the Wolf

He stands on a snow-covered slope, head arched toward the moon. His cry pierces the valleys and echoes for miles. It is a cry that has inspired legends, fueled myths, stirred up fear and loathing.

He is the "big, bad wolf" of nursery stories. He is the fierce predator who circles the camp. He is the enemy, the invader, the spoiler.

And he is the most maligned of creatures. He is carnivorous, yes, but so are most humans. He is also a faithful monogamous spouse to his mate. She is a devoted mother, playing with her pups, teaching them the ways of the wild. They are both community creatures with an intricate social webbing.

Lone Wolves

Young "lone wolves" eventually leave their pack, venturing out into the wilderness—solitary figures seeking new territory and a possible mate. Theirs is a heroic quest, for all they have known from youth has been the den, the pack and the communal hunt. Their trek may take them over a four hundred square mile territory.

The Hunt

The wolf pack hunts what they need. Faithful to their instincts, they trek through the winter snows, following the herds. Their lives too are an everyday adventure and challenge.

All things considered, theirs is a fair fight; not so when they are the prey—they are hunted and hounded from airplanes and helicopters, shot like fish in a barrel.

Humans seem to find it easy to hate the wolves, to despise their ways. Why? Could it be because we cannot bear to face and free up the wild wolf man or the wild woman who lives beneath the frozen surfaces of our own lives?

We are not so different from the wolf and the pack as we might think. In fact, we may be projecting our own dysfunctions and winter calamities upon this ancient "enemy."

CONSIDER:

Winter challenges the wolf pack. The search for food will take the pack into the face of gales with subzero windchills, over ice, through snow fields in relentless pursuit. Have you experienced

> ...the windchill of opposition,
> ...the ice of prejudice,
> ...the freezing out of misunderstanding?

Sometimes in the wolf pack there is a struggle for dominance. There is a change of roles after such a struggle. Have you experienced

> ...the stress of family dysfunction,
> ...the anguish of divorce,
> ...the pain of separation,
> ...the ache from a straying, prodigal relative,
> ...the dissonance from sibling conflicts?

Sometimes in the wolf pack there is a scarcity of caribou or an overrun of territory—too many wolves, not enough prey. Have you experienced

> ...unemployment,
> ...down-sizing,
> ...friction with fellow workers?

Often in the wolf pack there is movement, change of climate, tough running in their pursuit of moving prey. Have you experienced

> ...moving from the familiar to the unfamiliar,
> ...stress from a rapid pace and increasing demands,

...confusion, as the demands of our culture
accelerate with change?

Sooner or later, the "lone wolf" strays out from the pack and howls against the moon? Have your experienced

...isolation,
...loneliness,
...alienation?

There is an energy in the wolf that sees them through the worst of their snowy days and frozen nights. Their call from the wild is one of exuberance: "We are here! We belong here! We shall endure! We shall overcome!"

Our human call from our wilderness needs to be no less confident.

A Wolf Prayer

Creator God,
>are not my deepest powers damned up? frozen over?

There are times when I feel listless,
>made inert by repetitious days and long winter nights.

I wonder if there is life beyond Monday night football
>or milling at the mall?

It's easy to be simply a spectator of life,
>dazed and dulled.

The consumer society can swallow my soul.
I am programmed to be passionate about
>Bud Lite, little leagues, small advances in the stock market,
>and little else.

Life can too easily become a monitor—
>hard drives, soft drives, cathode tubes.

It is to be viewed, reviewed, instantly replayed,
>recorded, canned, put on the shelf.

It is not just cold outside;
>I seem frozen within.

Never so much sex, never so much action—
>up there on the screen—
>and so little passion within.

Let me befriend the wolf within,
>the wild energy of my own life force,
>my zest for life, my alertness of spirit.

Let me make the move,
>shake the springs,
>reawaken my wild dynamism from slumber.

Let me own my own imagination,
>   dream a better dream,
>   howl at the moon
>   and seek my bliss.
Help me to be alert to the direction
>   where a prize lies waiting for my prowl.

Let me be passionate about compassion,
>   for I share my trek
>   with all the human pack.
Like the wolf,
>   we are both the hunters,
>   and the hunted.

Let me lope with the wolf,
>   for life is an adventure,
>   and we must make tracks across the snow.

Image: The wolf on a snow-clad hill howling at the moon. Pray for some wolf energy in your own frozen, getting-nowhere days.

Journal: To melt the ice in my life, I need to...

Chapter Five

Praying with the Rain Forest,
Coral Reef and Sister Water
and Redwoods

Prayers for Healing Times

Praying with the Rain Forest

Lament of the Rain Forest Pygmies

The forest is Mother and Father because it gives us all the things we need...food, clothing, shelter, warmth...and affection. We are the children of the forest. When it dies, we die.

> Mary Batten, *The Tropical Forest, Ants, Animals and Plants*

Beyond the rain forests, we are disconnected. We are out of sync. We are sick, and we need to be healed. We are not only sometimes burdened with anxieties and depressions, but our very bodies are infected from our own soiled nests.

...We are in need of a fountain of healing
...We are the arsonists of the rain forests...and we burn
...We are the polluters of the streams...and we gag
...We are the poisoners of the air...and we choke
...We are the looters of the ozone...and we bake
...We are the poisoners of the earth...and we hunger
...We bite the hand that would feed us
...We spoil the beauty that would ennoble us
...We curse the creatures that would bless us
...We soil our own nest
...We are in need of a fountain of healing.

A Fable of Life and Healing

Once upon a time, a youth who wanted to be young forever set out on a vision quest to discover the fountain of youth. After searching through low deserts, peering into mine shafts and over high mountaintops, traveling across the great plains of America, the flood plains of the Nile and plodding at the edges of the rain forests, he returned tired, stressed and wounded in spirit.

So he approached an ancient wise one and said, "I have not found the fountain of youth. How can I find the great source of healing?"

The old wise one was silent for awhile and then replied: "Search for the living and healing creatures that are deep in the earth and closest to the stars. They have open arms and many hands which motion to you. Find the creatures that fade, die and then rise again. They and their smaller companions want to heal and purify. They will cool you in the heat and shelter you in the wind. Do not be dismayed by their long trunks and rough hides. At their very core, they possess radiating holy circles, mandalas— the universal symbols of wholeness and healing. Find these creatures. Treat them as friends and you will discover healing."

And so the youth went off in search of healers. He asked the elephant, who replied, "Yes, I have a rough trunk, but it will fade and die." He asked the snake, who replied, "Yes, my skin fades and dies. I shed my skin and become new again. And I am close to the earth but not, alas, to the sky." He asked the giraffe. "I am close to the sky but not deep in the earth." He asked the kangaroo. "I have a healing circle in my pouch, but I have no long trunk, nor rough hide."

Having searched over the earth, the youth returned to the old wise one seated under an ancient oak tree. "Wise one, tell me more that I might find the healing creatures."

The wise one replied: "Long before the Native American healing medicine wheels, long before cathedrals and their wholistic, rose circular windows, long before Stonehenge, the healing circle was upon the earth. Blessed trees possess that circle at their very core. Friendly herbs grow at their feet and often possess good medicine. Long before man came with the sword, the chain-saw or the flaming torch, a healing circle of green girded the earth.

"These are the holy rain forests filled with mysteries and potential healings. When these forests are treated with reverence, they yield secrets of healing. When they are invaded, trashed, despoiled, put to the torch, they yield their toxic secrets. You have a choice: choose death or choose life from the rain-forests. Perhaps it was the smoke of man's greed and foolishness hanging over the edges of the rain forest that kept you from discovering your fountain of healing. It may prevent others as well."

The Rain Forest—a Metaphor

The rain forest might well be the metaphor for the healing needed in our lives, for it is a "medicine chest" filled with many undiscovered medicinal treasures. Since such a large number of medicines derive from plant life, it may well be that cures for various current physical maladies are yet to be found in the vegetation-rich rain forests.

In the rain forest nature is in sync. Energy used is returned and recycled, and all the complex interactions work together to create and sustain life. Beyond the rain forests we depend on their processes for the oxygen we breathe.

Yet each year humans destroy, forever, millions of acres across the rain forest's life-promoting ecosystem. We do so at our own peril, for the rain forests with their abundance of both rainfall and filtered sunlight are also the most conducive areas for a vast variety of life-forms found on our earth. In one square mile of the Amazon rain forests three thousand species have been found thriving.

The Torch and the Forests

Rather than torching the rain forests, we might better light votive lights before these green "cathedrals" and pray for the wisdom to discover their secret and sacred powers.

Learning the Hard Way

Once, during a very healthy period in my own life, I walked into a boiler room that had little black wisps of smoke emitting from a large air-conditioning system. Within twenty-four hours I was hospitalized with severe industrial chemical poisoning.

I needed weeks of antibiotics, some of whose elements come from plants. I needed total rest. I needed clean air. After months of convalescence, when I first had the strength to walk to a car, a friend took me to a blue lake scattered with ducks and herons and surrounded by green trees. I sat by that lakeshore, thrilled by every sensation. The breeze whispered as it danced through the branches and gently brushed my cheek. I felt a moment of enchantment. I felt embraced.

I experienced that place in a deeper way than I had ever known a natural setting. It became an epiphany charged with energy. Everything before me was vibrant and teeming with life. At that moment, an insight welled up within me: After months of confinement, my soul demanded more than pills and boxed-in walls; it needed the nursing touch of nature. My eyes ached for the dreaminess of clouds and for all the shades of green that nature paints upon a hillside.

My spirit thirsted for living water. The rhythmic rippling of the lake at my feet was like a gentle massage for my aching spirit. No wonder Francis of Assisi could call water "beloved Sister Water" and the poet Gerard Manley Hopkins could say of all that I was experiencing:

> And for all of this, nature is never spent;
> There lives the dearest freshness deep down things.
>
> ("God's Grandeur")

At that moment, I became aware that creation often desires to heal us. That lesson is being validated by research. We now know that even gazing at beautiful natural scenes can have a healing effect on the human. In an article in *U.S. News* entitled "Nature Soothes Body and Soul" we learn that:

> The psyche's love of natural sciences can have a powerful healing effect on the human body. Roger Ulrich (environmental psychologist at Texas A&M University) found that patients who had gall bladder surgery for instance, recovered faster and needed fewer strong painkillers when they had a view of trees through their window rather than a brick wall....Clearly nature provides humans with more than just a pretty view.[3]

PRAYER OF THE RAIN FOREST

All-Wise Creator, help us to be attentive.
Your rain forest creates intricacy and balance.
    It has so much to offer our bodies, minds and spirits.
    It waits to heal us!
    It expresses affection.

We need to listen, to learn to be respectful.
If we become very still and reverent,
    it might speak to us in ways
    far more profound than cathedrals.

I need to listen to the words of affection
    that come from the heart of the rain forests...

I know about LIFE.
I have within me
some of the oldest forms of life on planet earth.
I am more favorable to abundant life
than any place on earth.

Some animals who live within me have immunity to viruses

that similar animals living beyond my boundaries succumb to.
What might you learn from this?

I may have within me
plants that will make good medicine for AIDS.
I may have vines that will strangle cancer.
I possess a balance of life-forms in a world out of balance,
a world teetering at the edge of ecocide.
Do not ignore my wisdom.

My leafy arms are linked together in a great green baldachino
that arches over the mystery of life.
Holy! Holy! Holy!

I join my prayer with the chorus from the rain-forest
    singing, cheetering, swaying, roaring "Yes!" to life.
I seek the fountain of healing,
    the tree of life, the circle's center.
This day I commend myself and all those I love
    to the great, pulsating life force
    that joins me to all creatures.
May my *Holy! Holy! Holy!* mean:
Whole! Healed! Hallowed!

Image: If your are down with a cold or recovering from a virus, besides your medicine and additional rest, picture yourself in a favorite soothing natural environment. You might even from time to time image a guardian angel leading a host of green friends out of the rain forest. See them gently pushing away infection. Welcome and relish such images. Repeat to yourself, "I am being healed" or "Guardian Angel, continue to help heal me." Imagine your body glowing with new strength.

In your TV or movie watching during convalescence, search out laughter, another strong medicine.

Journal: I need to learn from the rain forest...

PRAYING WITH THE CORAL REEF AND SISTER WATER

A coral reef in the sea is like an oasis in the desert....The result is the world's oldest ecosystem and what may be the most complex animal and plant community on earth, rivaled only by the tropical rain forest.

> Roberta and James Q. Wilson, *Watching Fishes,*
> *Life and Behaviour on the Coral Reefs*

Through the Discovery Channel, the photography of Jacques Costeau and the efforts of *National Geographic* we have available to us more discoveries about the hidden life of the sea than explorers like Columbus could have dreamed.

Photographs and movie footage of the coral reefs reveal a spectacle that rivals the Grand Canyon in beauty. Its teeming, exotic plant and fish life makes the array of Disney's imaginary characters seem paltry by comparison. Extravagant colors and lace-like designs reveal a hidden aquatic Garden of Eden.

WATER MEANS LIFE

The coral reef reminds us of our origins and the fecundity of our sister Holy Water. Our origins are in the ancient seas; our very bodies are composed mostly of water. Our first nine months were lived in the water of the womb.

The flowing waters of streams and rivers demand our extrovert attention and care. As far as we now know, planet earth is the only place in the universe to have flowing water. Water is the source of all life. Conversely, it is estimated that: "80% of all diseases in the developing world come from unsafe or polluted water."[4]

In the developed world, water is also essential for our well being. One expert, Dr. Ralph Herro, M.D. of the Herro Allergy Clinic in Phoenix testifies: "If we drank twice as much water, doctors would be seeing half as many patients."

DEEP WATER AND OUR INTROVERT ATTENTION

Deep water also symbolizes the unknown depths of our planet and of our psyche. Water as a symbol calls us to the deep, unseen wellsprings within each of us.

Just as the sea and especially the coral reefs are inhabited in their depths by amazing and exotic creatures, so too the sea-like depths of our own unconscious can bring forth new and unsuspected treasures. Each of us, Jacques Costeau-like, can take on the challenging yet enormously fruitful work of inner exploration. Whether through depth psychology, contemplative prayer or creativity, which always brews in the dark, we need to discover those untapped resources of insight, intuition and vision that can lead us into the new millennium.

PRAYING WITH SISTER WATER

An Extrovert Prayer with Revitalizing Water

For my friend Sister Water I give thanks
>...for rainy days,
>...for the kiss of rain upon the earth,
>...for its soft drumbeat upon my rooftop,
>...for the "swish, swish" of the windshield wipers,
>...for bobbing umbrellas and yellow raincoats,
>...for children splashing in puddles,
>...for water beads like pearls upon my window pane,
>...for the cascading, tingling rivulets of my shower,
>...for the soothing, sensuous immersion of my bath,
>...for the mountain stream—
>>>like a lover rushing to be with me
>...for the cool, clear drinking water—

that actually becomes me!

I pray for strength and healing from pure water:
>...from holy wells in the womb of mother earth,
>...from flowing rivers, lifelines on planet earth,
>...from melting snows and crystal streams,
>...from saunas, whirlpools and swimming pools,
>...from holy water upon my lips,
>...from soothing water washing my body/spirit.

An Introvert Prayer with Holy Water

I pray with deep waters:

Let the deep water, filled with unseen possibilities,
>touch the mysterious unknown in me.
Let the water, sun-splashed by countless sparkling reflections,
>remind me of my own countless possibilities.

Let me plumb the hidden treasures of my own deep images,
>my imagination swarming like a coral reef with exotic beauty.
Let my subtle mind freely swim about
>for there is much to be discovered.

Let the rippling waves remind me
>of the ebb and flow in my life journey.
Let water's depth move me to plumb the depths
>of my creativity where surprising creatures play.

Let me be quiet now with Sister Water.
>Let her depth speak to me, her beauty console me.
Let her healing presence
>seep into the arid cracks in my soul.

Image: Your favorite water scene; take some quiet time to just be with your friend, Holy Water. Let it refresh you.

Journal: In my own very depths there is an undiscovered coral reef of indescribable beauty; may I...

Praying with the Redwoods

A Guided Meditation

(If you possess a tape recorder, you might record this meditation with its proper pauses and then use the recording in your prayer.)

Relax. Prepare yourself to take an imaginary journey through the ancient, sacred redwood forests of California. Read very slowly and with the eye of your imagination. Pause at each ... mark to savor the images in your mind and soul.

It is dusk and you have been hiking. You decide to take a shortcut through the redwood forest on the way back to your car. Behold the majestic trees towering before you.... As you move and weave your way around the gigantic trunks of the ancient trees, darkness is descending. Clouds begin to pull a curtain across the moon. A soft rain is filtering down through the overarching forest. Let your imagination take you there. You stand for awhile in silence....

Now you move on. You make your way through the magnificent woods as you go deeper into the forest. Then you realize that you are lost. You are not sure which way to go in order to return to the highway. So you keep trudging along, hoping that your movement will lead you out. After awhile, you notice a little glow ahead of you. You peer ahead and see its dim light filtering through the forest.... You head toward this solitary light in the dark....

Soon you come upon the most gigantic of redwoods. It is hollowed out at its base, and within its hollow you discover an ancient hooded figure seated near a small fire.... The stranger smiles at you, "Come in, friend. Sit by my little campfire. Have a cup of brew (You savor the taste...)."

Your host speaks again, "You wonder about this hollowed space? It is caused by ancient fires. Here in the redwoods, Brother

Fire arrives through lightning strikes and is actually a friend and companion to the trees. They need him to burn away the brush and make room. Here, even fire is in balance with earth and sun and rain. But rest a bit. Enjoy the warmth and your cup of cheer...."

After a long silence, you are moved to ask, "But who are you, and what do you do here?"

"Oh, just call me Friend of the Forest. What do I do here? I walk among friends. I read books and I read trees. Let me share something with you that I just read." He picks up a book and reads aloud:

> You should walk as often as possible among plants that have a wonderful aroma, spending a considerable amount of time every day among such things.
>
> In a former time, exercise was inseparable from experiencing the world, walking through it, smelling it, and feeling it sensually, even as the heart got its massage from the exertion of the walk.[5]

"You can't jog through the forest (or through life) and still fully experience every moment. The plants and all living things have too many gifts to give you. Sometimes you need to stop and take them in. Be receptive; receive their hospitality, just as you've received mine.

"Now, I know you want to find your way out of the forest, so I will be your guide. But first you must choose a knapsack," he says, pointing to a pile of knapsacks. "Notice how each one has a label. One says *stress*, another *worry*, another *anxiety*, another *haunting bad memories*. One of them is probably yours, the one you usually carry. If none of those labels fit you, then take this marker and write on one of the knapsacks the name of the burden you usually carry.... Now, pick up your own knapsack." (In your imagination do so; feel its heaviness, tighten its straps.)

"Let us go out into the forest; I will show you the way." It has stopped raining. The full moon is now out—its glow filters down upon the forest floor and forms lacy patterns....

After walking awhile, Friend of the Forest pauses at a scraggly ancient redwood. "Look at this grandfather. He was here when Caesar was in Rome and Jesus was in Galilee. He is a relative with an ancient wisdom. I read the other day that Emerson said the greatest delight the woods can offer us is to suggest an occult relationship between humans and green things. I believe these ancient ones are truly friends to us. Not only are they awesome in their reach to the heavens, they clean the air we breathe and reach out to us with care and affection. I feel at home here."

You walk along beside the bank of a swift flowing stream. You start to climb at a place where the stream hollows out a gorge. "Let's stop a moment," says Friend of the Forest. "Do you like diamonds? Take a long, loving look at Sister Water below. In the moonlight she sparkles like a million jewels.... She's also rushing down the hill with passion. She hurries to wash us, to quench our thirst, to share our journey. We might pause and thank her for her favor.... Ah! Let's move on now."

Soon you come to a crest; the stream is far below. There is a small footbridge across the gorge. It is anchored to a redwood on the other side. Friend of the Forest points to the fragile-looking bridge. "You can cross over here. The path beyond will lead you out of the woods. You know, you sometimes have to travel a long way through the woods before you know where you've been or where you are going. But when you find your path in the midst of the dark wood, it will lead you home.

"Before you go on, you must lay down your burden. The bridge is too fragile for both of you. Reach around and unsnap your pack. Now look once more at its label. What does it say?... Now gently place it on the ground. You may cross. Peace be with you."

As you proceed across the gently swaying bridge, Friend of the Forest calls after you, "Look at the water below.... When you reach the other side, take a good last look at the craggy redwood. You might thank it for giving you a lifeline over the stream. Give it a smile, or even a pat for just being there."

As you turn and wave to Friend of the Forest, your new friend smiles and says, "You have walked through the forest, you have smelled it, you have felt it. You have received its affection and some of its ancient healing wisdom. You have gently laid down your own inner storm. Let the earth love you, the trees protect you, the water renew you. Walk with care and befriend creation. If you do, she will lavish upon you many blessings. Go now, but return to this forest when you need to be regenerated and reintegrated. Remember, your journey has been a healing prayer. Take time daily to journey on a healing path."

Image: The redwood, tall, straight, a symbol of strength.

Journal: The healing I seek...

Chapter Six

Praying with Home Angels,
Cat
and Dog

Prayers for the Home Times

Home Angels

Just when it feels like it's hopeless,
and I'll never make it alone,
I hear the voices of angels,
tenderly calling me home.

Traditional hymn

O God, send your holy angel from heaven—
to watch over, to cherish, to protect and to bless
all who dwell in this house.

I said this prayer when I visited seventy-six-year-old Alice in her small apartment. We shared laughter, stories and prayer. She was sitting up during our time together but would soon be in a coma. Before I left, a perky squirrel greeted Alice by tapping on the glass of her sliding kitchen door. Alice introduced this bright-eyed, furry creature as one of her daily "friends and companions."

The very next night, the angels came and took Alice home. But Alice already knew an "angel" in her friendly squirrel. Those creatures that enliven our dwellings, that catch our attention, that elicit our care, that deliver messages of life and growth—I call them "home angels."

Angel Messengers

Unlike Alice, who was at home until she died, increasingly more and more Americans spend their last years away from home.

"Care Centers" sprout up in every community, opening their doors to burgeoning numbers of the elderly. These buildings are often similar. Spidery arms reach out from a central core. Long corridors with their polished floors create a labyrinth of hard surfaces which can be echo chambers for groans and cries. Time can plod a slow course through these halls. Visitors to a care center will often observe a few patients sitting in the halls, staring vacantly. More often than not, one patient will cry out, "Home! I want to go home!"

Not so for Genevieve, age eighty-seven, whom time has slowed but not dulled. Although she does not get outside too often, she can sometimes be found in her wheelchair with a smile on her face, listening to the chatter and song of beautiful birds. She spends many happy moments near the aviary which occupies a central point in her care center.

Many care centers for the elderly and incapacitated have installed aviaries or aquariums. The aviaries filled with brightly colored birds provide symphonies of birdsong. The birds and the residents share a common confinement. The birds' singing not only soothes the residents, but it can remind them that beauty can be found even in confinement. This is a message worthy of angels.

When an aquarium is present, it offers a connection to the great flow of life—a coming home to our very origins. The brilliantly colored fish with their graceful movements contrast a human existence that is static, bound up, imprisoned.

Angel Guides

In angel lore, angels are not only messengers, they are also guides. Yet no angel ever guided a human being better than Michael does for Cynthia. Cynthia is sightless. She sits in a restaurant with Michael, a handsome German shepherd, curled up at her feet. Michael is a powerful animal quite capable of creating a stir, but he is in harness, and this is a working day. There will be no nonsense from Mike. When Cynthia finishes her meal, he will unwind, get up and patiently lead her through the busy restaurant. He moves with as much grace and know-how as the most experienced waiter employed there. Outside, he will guide Cynthia safely through crowds and traffic. Michael is no barker. He has no time for frivolity. He is a "home angel" gently guiding Cynthia home. Michael the Archangel could be proud that this gentle shepherd bears his name.

OKLAHOMA CITY

In the terrible aftermath of the 1995 Oklahoma City bombing, after rescuers had sought the most easily reached survivors, the grim task of finding those still buried alive and the many dead was turned over to humankind's "best friends." Golden retrievers could be seen patiently sniffing through the rubble, possessing an affinity for human presence which no human could match. When they had done all they could do, it was left to heaven's angels to gently take home those whom the dogs could not find.

A VARIETY OF HOME ANGELS

There are many creatures who are helpers to humankind whom we might name our "home angels." It might be a cricket on the hearth, a singing bird, a swimming fish, a cat, a dog or a green houseplant, or even lightning bugs whose luminescence brightens summer evenings. I have two cacti and a sheaf of shamrocks. They are my home angels. Like good angels, their mission is to be emissaries of a divine word.

The shamrocks remind me of my roots, of Celtic spirituality which is earthy and three-dimensional. They deliver a message that I have a hearth because my ancestors passed on life and love in hard times. Like my ancestors who lived in mists and gentle rain, my shamrocks drink lots of water and survive just fine in the shade. They tell me that not every day can be sunny.

My cactus plants slow me down. They live simply, and they bring a message of steadfastness and patient growth. These are indeed the words of angels.

It is the work of angels to daily reveal words about the creator. Meister Eckhart, a great medieval mystic, explained it this way:

Every creature is a word of God.
If I spent enough time with the tiniest creature,
even a caterpillar—
I would never have to prepare a sermon,
so full of God is every creature....
every single creature is full of God
and is a book about God![6]

A Home Angels Prayer

"O God, send your holy angels from heaven,
    to watch over, to cherish, to protect and to bless
    all who dwell in this house."

May the wag of a tail, the arching of a back,
    the flutter of a wing or the swish of fur
    be an angel sign of content.

May the silent company of plants
    give rootedness and earthiness
    to home, to hearth and to hands.

May the trees near my dwelling
    be "angel guardians"
    around my door.

May all the angels of my home
    brighten the days,
    and calm the nights.

May they give insight, O God,
    into your nature and your ways,
    and remind me of your care and loving protection.

Image: The living creatures that deliver messages to your house.
Pray with gratitude for their messages of...

Journal: The blessings I seek for my home are...

Praying with the Cat

Cats are "in." Not only are they treasured pets in many homes, they also strut their stuff as actors and actresses in commercials, movies and plays. The Broadway musical *Cats,* featuring humans in cat disguises, turned out to be a cataclysmic success that continues to entertain. Out in Los Angeles real cats can prepare for their stage debut. They attend Cat Schools to catapult them into stardom as performers. There they learn hisses and costume tolerance. They even graduate.

In cities like Miami, "biz cats" are catching on. Their jobs include everything from patrolling a fish warehouse to creating a leisurely ambiance in a travel agency or calming patients in a doctor's office. Doctor Adair Alspach, owner of an animal hospital, attests to the benefits of cat presence. She cites studies showing that some people's blood pressure drops significantly when stroking a cat and that cats are effective mood changers when introduced into nursing homes or centers for autistic children.[7]

Back at home, our own "Garfields" reign supreme. Equipped with two sets of vocal chords, one to "meow" and another to "growl" they are not hesitant to reveal their needs. Yet in many other ways they cater to our needs as well.

CATS

There are biz cats and copycats,
fat cats, catcalls, and pratfalls,
catnips and catnaps,
alley cats, bob cats and wildcats.
There are cat houses and frat houses,
and at Northwestern, Kentucky or Kansas State,
Wildcats are where it's at.

Cats can glide ever so smoothly.
Experts at relaxing,
they preen and meow and prowl.
Slinky and laid back,
self-sufficient, they arch and stretch.
Watch how they watch you.
Whiskers like antennae at the dew line,
sense and search and keep in touch.

Be watchful for the time when this casual observer seizes
the moment and strikes. No wonder that any quick and agile
movement is described as catlike. After the hunt, the cat purrs
and then curls into catatonic slumber.

CAT PRAYER

I come home from my prowl,
    inching my way through traffic snarls.
Every muscle taut, tensed,
    wound up tighter than a ball of yarn.
High strung from too many demands,
    I almost need more than nine lives,
    to get everything done.
I carry home with me strain and stress
    from trying to meet goals and deadlines.
I am expected to be a working tiger,
    yet sometimes I wonder:
    Am I the hunter or the hunted?

May I learn from the cat
    to totally unwind, to shed my cares
    as easily as a cat sheds its hair.
Slow stretching will be my body prayer,
    letting out a primal "Meow,"
    curling and twisting my arms.
Arching my back,
    letting go of this day's burdens,
    I open to the creative flow of leisure.
Creator God of fish, fur and four-legged friends,
    when your work was done,
    even you stretched and rested—on the seventh day.
Bless my journey to the couch
    for a luxurious catnap.
    Purr!

Image: A cat, like the one in the prayer, returning home from a long night's hunt and curling up for a nap in a favorite sunny spot.

Journal: My prayer of contentment is...*or* I need to rest from...

Praying with the Dog

In Homer's epic, *The Odyssey*, Odysseus returns home from the Trojan Wars and is not recognized by any of the humans who knew him. It is only Argos, a faithful dog weakened unto death by his master's absence, who affirms his presence. The old dog, prostrate on a dung heap, musters a last surge of strength, wagging his tail and dropping his ears. The unconditional love, devotion and loyalty of such a dog might well challenge our family and love relationships. Can we do as well?

Shep's Story

In northern Montana, in the heart of the range country, there is a monument to a real canine who waited long years for his master's return. Fort Benton is an old railhead and riverboat town near the headwaters of the Missouri River. Lewis and Clark passed through, followed by fur traders, cowboys and sheepherders. Down by the river there is a series of plaques recalling their passages and exploits, but up above them all, high on a bluff, is a monument to an old sheepdog. The dog's statue looks out over the river and the railroad track, always watching for a special train. The inscription below the dog's statue reads:

Shep's Vigil

In August, 1936, a casket containing a sheepherder's body was loaded on a baggage cart here, headed East for burial. A dog, of collie strain, watched with anxious eyes. He was to be there to meet every train, year after year. Conductor Ed Shields by 1939 pieced the dog's story together, linking Shep with the body shipped that August day. With the real story known, Shep became famous. Many, many well-intended offers to adopt him were gently declined. Friends knew Shep's sole aim was to keep his vigil. Shep died Jan. 12, 1942, slipping on the tracks before an incoming train. His passing was mourned by all who knew his story. He was laid to rest atop the bluff above the depot. His funeral was attended by hundreds. Rev. Ralph Underwood took as his theme Senator George Vest's "Eulogy on the Dog," a tribute to a dog's faithfulness to his master which Shep so fully exemplified.

My Own Golden Retriever

When I was twelve, our family took a long summer trip to the Northwest. We had to leave Joe, my golden retriever, on a farm while we were away. Upon our return three months later, the farmer said that Joe was not around the farmyard, but that we probably would find him if we took a walk out on a nearby gravel road. As I walked down the road, a figure appeared on the horizon. As it came closer, its familiar golden coat shone in the sun. At first Joe was walking; then he cocked his ears and started to trot. When he finally got our scent, he broke into a run. Never in all of my travels have I received such a greeting as I got that day. When he reached us, he leapt and barked and his tail flew in all directions. He was like a berserk symphony conductor leading the finale of Beethoven's Ninth.

The reunion of a boy and his dog—perhaps no kinship with any animal can surpass it. I remember getting Joe when he was a pup and I was a skinny nine-year-old. When we went to look at the litter, the owner pointed to the scrawny pup in the corner and said, "You probably don't want that one; he's the runt of the litter." But I did want him. Was it because I was the runt kid in our neighborhood? Or, did he choose me?

We grew up together. I treasure a picture of me in a stocking cap, and—with dirty knuckles clearly showing—my hand on his shoulder. On his face in that photo is the timeless expression of the retriever, always ready to fetch for his master. We would run together, play together, wrestle together. He might growl now and then, but he would never bite. (It did not surprise me when a recent study showed that of all dogs the golden retriever bites the least.[8])

One day, he dragged himself home, victim of a hit-and-run. The vet splinted up his broken leg in an aluminum frame cast. He dragged it around patiently until the day he knew it was time for it to be removed—and then he chewed it all off.

I went away to college, and every time I came home I could expect that same homecoming jubilation from my old friend Joe. Then, one semester, I returned and he was not there. My fiercely faithful companion from childhood had died. Even today, every time I see a golden retriever, with its alert eyes and gentle face, Joe is there. Memories come back of an only child, a runt kid with dirty knuckles and a beautiful golden dog, ever loyal and devoted, always retrieving and returning to my side. We should all be fortunate enough to have such a friend as Joe.

MAN'S BEST FRIEND

An essential ingredient of any friendship is communication. No question in my mind, Joe and I communicated as friends. When a national news magazine ran an article which questioned the possibility of animals grasping human words, a golden retriever owner responded by letter:

> No one who has ever owned and hunted with a golden or labrador retriever will believe the statement that "It's very unlikely that a dog...actually understands the words its owner speaks to it." ["What Animals Say to Each Other," June 5]. I have had two golden retrievers and now have a labrador retriever. I have found that dogs not only understand full sentences but are more effective communicators than at least one lawyer I often try my cases against. Their other qualities would exhaust all of the things a Boy Scout is supposed to be.[9]

THE GOLDEN RETRIEVER

He *is* a scout. He is also a land rover and a fearless swimmer, an all-purpose dog for all seasons. He's certainly a dog with some qualities much needed by humans in our season of "I'll take yours and make it mine." When all around us we observe corporate gobblings, metro muggings, white-collar banditry, thieves, gangs and thugs, and sometimes unreturned love—this golden-furred express agent returns everything!

Head held high, he splashes into deep waters. He surges forward with supreme confidence, loyal to his breeding destiny. No matter how far he swims out into deep water, he will always circle and come around to home again where he gently lets go of the hunter's prize. Going out, turning, coming back again, letting go, he is a golden swirl of bobbing energy. And whatever he returns and drops to the ground is unscarred by his possession. His swimming paws are those of a worker who has mastered his craft. His gentle jaws reveal an instinct for generosity, an inbreeding of devotion.

COMING HOME

The heart of the retriever is fiercely devoted to "coming home again." It is the story of this dog's life. It's our human story too. Coming home for us humans means reconnecting over and over with that intricate web of relationships where love and friendship are given generously and gratefully received. "Home is where the heart is." A cliche? Not really. A grateful heart is always at home.

A Retriever Homecoming Prayer

The retriever—a homecoming dog for all seasons,
    living reminder of faithfulness and devotion.
O God, you who are the "hound of heaven,"
    your unconditional love pursues my busy heart.
May your loving pursuit remind me to cherish
    all that is home: loved ones, friends, my deepest dreams.

Home at last from making the plunge of this day,
    sometimes swimming against the current.
Let the waves of my life experiences settle,
    so I may settle into what is true.
I am grateful to come back home again,
    home to my space, home to my heart,

It is in the "turning, turning,
    that we come 'round right."*
Bread cast upon the waters,
    return to nourish me.
Let me retrieve
    the presence of those who love me.

May I recall forgotten kindnesses,
    golden reveries drifting to awareness.
At the end of this day as I arrive home,
    I too am like a retriever letting go.
Dropping burdens at your feet,
    help me to take time to be playful as a pup.

from Quaker Dance

Image: Shep, Joe or one of your favorite creatures. Take in its beauty and grace, its playfulness, its affectionate greetings, its devoted sitting at your side. Be grateful for such creatures or some human relationship of unconditional love. Pray about the messages these images bear...

Journal: Such devoted creatures move me to...

Chapter Seven

Praying with the Horse,
Dolphin
and Leviathan

Prayers for Rejoicing Times

> The animal motif is usually symbolic of man's primitive
> and instinctual nature....In the religions and religious art of
> practically every race, animal attributes are ascribed to the
> supreme gods or the gods are represented in animals.
>
> Carl Jung, *Man and His Symbols*

Human beings have a close affinity to animals. Their instinctual
natures, their swift and graceful movements, their ability to survive
and overcome great obstacles, their bodily earthiness, all inspire
a certain effervescent joy in humans. When we human beings
triumph or achieve success, we often celebrate in a very bodily,
animal fashion. It is not surprising, for we are not just rational,
we are rational animals.

JUBILEE

We sometimes jump and dance for joy. Jubilee, jubilation,
joy enter into our lives in so many different ways—the joy of a
honeymoon, the birth of a child, the celebration of birthdays,
anniversaries, reunions, graduations, successes, promotions,
family celebrations, deep experiences of beauty.

Creativity and a sense of accomplishment with our work
can also bring a joyful satisfaction. So can contemplation and
prayer. And sometimes our joy arises from very simple causes—
a beautiful day, a good meal, a friendly smile. Notice children
who skip down the sidewalk. They simply enjoy being alive! They
are exhibiting what the French call *joie de vivre*, the joy of living.

Animal Symbolism

Sometimes our celebrations of joy are charged with mythic energy, signaling the triumph of a just cause against an infamous one. I have etched in my memory a "day of infamy," December 7, 1941, the attack on Pearl Harbor. I was a ten-year-old playing with my dog Joe on the front lawn. The grass was brown, no snow. I remember coming in the house and hearing the crackle of the radio announcing what was in effect the beginning of World War II.

I also remember quite clearly the jubilation that occurred in 1945 on V-E Day, and the events leading up to it. Animal symbolism emerged from those momentous events which helped to highlight a mythic struggle between good and evil. Hitler's redoubt on a mountain top in Bavaria was called his eagle's nest. A fierce eagle perched upon the swastika. His tanks which swept through Europe were named "Tigers."

Cavalry to the Rescue*

At the Battle of the Bulge, when American tanks dashed to Bastogne, Belgium to break the Tiger tanks' siege of the surrounded Allied troops, they were the last vestige of the old cavalry. Their embroidered shoulder patches bore the yellow shield tracing back to the old-time yellow kerchiefs of the frontier cavalry. It was fitting that the descendents of the old horse soldiers would race to the rescue. As a result, the Battle of the Bulge became Hitler's last gasp.

The First Armored Division which also helped rout the Nazis still today wears a yellow cavalry patch with a horse's head emblazoned on it. Later in World War II these armored columns would liberate wretched concentration camps and their starving occupants and set the eagle free from the swastika.

---

* *"Cavalry to the rescue" remains a Western myth. Sitting Bull would take exception. However, his brave descendants were among the "cavalry" freeing Europe in 1945.*

In the closing days of the war one last symbolic liberation took place. The U.S. Third Army set free from Hitler's grasp the white Lippizaner show horses of Austria, a national treasure and symbol of grace and freedom.

JUBILATION

I remember the V-E Day that followed. We knew the war in Europe was finished and it would only be a matter of time before the largest war in the history of humankind would end. On V-E Day, without any urging, people dropped what they were doing and converged on downtown. Church bells clanged in jubilation. Auto horns honked. Any servicemen or -women appearing on the streets would be hugged and kissed by as many people as would find them. People danced in the streets, jumped, yelled and slapped one another's backs. Some of the more adventurous climbed streetlight poles. Near the stockyards district a cattleman rode a horse right into a bar.

Since 1929, the world had been wearied by a stock market crash, a long depression, a world war. 1945 was perhaps the greatest jubilee year of the twentieth century. When V-J Day (Victory in Japan) followed, the euphoria of the end of the war once again made the words of the ancient prophet Isaiah fresh and hope filled:

> These will hammer their swords into plowshares, their spears into sickles...the wolf lives with the lamb, the panther lies down with the kid, calf and lion cub feed together, with a little boy to lead them. The cow and the bear make friends. Their young lie down together. The infant plays over the cobra's hole; into the viper's lair the young child puts his hand (Is. 1: 4, 11: 6-8).

ANIMAL MOTIFS

Hitler's Tiger tanks and the U.S. Army horse insignia are only recent illustrations of animal symbolism taking on mythic meaning. Our affinity to animals and animal symbolism is universal and predates written history. Animal motifs and pictures have been found on cave walls between 10,000 and 60,000 B.C.! Greek mythology particularly is filled with animal figures. Fairy tales from all times and traditions have animals befriending humans and bringing them joy.

The ancient signs of the zodiac refer to animal figures as do some symbols of the enneagram. The Chinese zodiac has twelve different animal signs relating to various years of birth. In the vision quests of many Native Americans, the questing young visionary would seek to encounter an animal or bird. Identifying with the animal creature would be the catalyst for initiation from childhood into adulthood.

In the Judeo-Christian era, when John the Baptist announced Jesus, he proclaimed, "Behold the Lamb of God!" Jesus compared himself to a mother hen wanting to gather her chicks. King Herod is referred to as an old fox. Mark is symbolized by the lion, Luke by the ox and John by the soaring eagle. In the beautiful words of Isaiah quoted above, the prophet uses the image of the wolf, bear and lion and other animals living together to describe a world at peace.

As Old as Ancient History, As New as Monday Night

Each Monday night in the fall of the year, a modern ritual takes place. Millions of American males as well as their wives and sweethearts seek a vision on the TV tube and identify closely with Bears, Dolphins, Seahawks, Cardinals, Eagles, Broncos, Lions, Rams, Bengals, Colts, Falcons and Ravens. They often display their totem images on T-shirts, jerseys and jackets.

And when the professional athletes on the screen perform with animal grace and achieve great triumphs, there is usually primitive rejoicing. On the screen, the athletes leap, high-five, bear hug, dance and preen. In many sports bars the observers do some of the same.

Animal images, then, are quite natural for the rejoicing times of our own lives. The head-tossing horse, the breaching whale, the playful dolphin all speak to our deepest instincts to survive, to overcome, to triumph and to leap with joy.

Praying with the Horse

The Journey of the Horse

We grew from midget-size to man-size and beyond.
In shaggy winter coats,
    we trotted down frozen Mongolian steppes.

We pulled Caesar's chariots to the rim of the Empire.
We hoisted knights seeking the Grail.
We put our shoulders to the plow and furrowed Europe.
We bore the heavy armor of the conquistadors.

We circled Custer at Little Bighorn,
    rejoicing with the tribes,
    rearing back in jubilee.
From express posts,
    we raced breakneck across the plains,
    bearing myths and legends.
We witnessed the last charge of the last cavalryman, George Patton,
    liberating Lippizaners, ermine clad
    for the requiem of the Reich.

As we bore J.F.K. to rest,
    the clatter of our hooves shattered the silence,
    our cadence signaling grace, carrying on.
When unsaddled from Apocalypse,
    we shall throw back our heads,
    rejoicing with all that's free.

The Mythic Horse

Pegasus, the winged horse created from the blood of Medusa, caused the spring of Hippocrates to flow by a stroke of his hoof. The image of this soaring creature speaks of freedom, resilience, new life and rejoicing.

The Ancient Celts

In ancient Celtic lore, horses held a mythic grasp on the imagination. Their exuberance matched the wild energy of the Celts. In pre-Christian times, a tribal leader might assume his role as chief by attempting intercourse with a white mare. A very earthy people indeed! The Celts were a people close to the wildness of their beloved horses. *The Little Book of Celtic Wisdom* describes Cuchulainn, the greatest mythic hero of pre-Christian Ireland, as:

> Fast moving on the plain like mountain mist...
> With the speed of the hare on level ground.
> The fast step—the joyful step
> Of the horses coming towards us
> Like snow hewing the slopes![10]

For the ancient Celts, horses were companions in life, and sometimes mourners at death. In *The Flowering of Ireland* Katherine Sherman writes that before Cuchulainn's last battle his horse "The Grey Mare of Macha" sensed his master's doom and shed big round tears of blood. When his master lay mortally wounded, the valiant horse made three circular charges around him, slaying 170 of his enemies in the forays.

In Our Day

Only when Hitler's panzers rolled over the Polish cavalry did the horse's glory diminish, and yet even now all mechanized hordes must measure their force in *horsepower*. Overshadowed, the horse might have passed from our gaze, but it has not. For the horse cannot be separated from our spirit. When catching sight of a horse, how can there not stir a sense of kinship? We have been too close, our destinies intertwined for too many eons, not to intuit a bond.

I remember standing in a pasture in County Sligo in Ireland. In the twilight time before sundown, for nearly an hour, I tried to coax a magnificent stallion to come to the fence line. I nicknamed him *Cuchulainn*. He would take two steps forward and then one back. He let me know that he might be fenced, but he still was free.

There is something special about such a horse that can stir our blood. We are captivated by the mane unfurling in the breeze, the exuberance, the free spirit, the head thrown to the wind, the wild eyes, the rollicking abandon of the gallop. Even in concrete cities where horse flesh cannot be seen, their presence still bursts out through TV images of Clydesdales or thoroughbreds, their glinting shoes airborne.

Even the bobbing heads on the merry-go-round—as they run, run, run, turn, turn, turn, around and around seem to proclaim: Rejoice! Rejoice! Rejoice!

An Equine Prayer

Divine Spirit of power and free-flight,
    today my spirit rides
with the mustangs of the unfenced west,
    unbridled from burdens and expectations.
I sense at the core of my being
    a freedom and an inner strength.

          I shall not be driven from without,
             but rather empowered from within.
          Unburdened from all oppressive riders,
             not roped in,
             spurs unloosed,
          I am like Pegasus taking flight.

I rejoice with the wind!
    I move with grace,
    rearing back with laughter.
Glory and praise for such a time,
    for such a place!

Image: The mustang, free on the range, alert, fully alive. Pray out of the beauty and exhilaration of that scene.

Journal: In this energetic time...

Praying with the Dolphin

Blessed be! Blessed Be! Blessed Be!
Dolphins leaping
Whales breaching
Horses racing
Falcons diving
Bears rumbling
Rams butting
Seahawks flocking
Cardinals singing
Colts frolicking
Eagles soaring
Lions roaring
Broncos bucking
Children skipping
Lovers kissing
Friends sharing
Lame leaping
Blind seeing
Brides blushing
Grooms glowing
Parades strutting
Dancers pirouetting
Birthday candles blazing
Soldiers returning
Spirits lifting
Sick healing
Clowns laughing
Hearts beating
Tides rolling
Sun rising
Fortunes shifting!
Blessed be! Blessed be! Blessed be!

The Exuberant Jumper

In Dingle Bay in County Kerry, Ireland, a gregarious dolphin once befriended the town and frolicked in its bay far from the normal haunts of dolphins. He even has a pub named after him.

In Australia, another friendly dolphin lifted an exhausted swimmer in danger of drowning and gently nudged her toward the shore.

In the Caribbean, sleek dolphins play their leaping games in the wakes of cruise liners.

Off the coast of New England, a mother dolphin, after eleven months of waiting, gently lifts her newborn to the surface for its first gulp of air. Other baby dolphins glide alongside their mothers, sometimes at high speeds with little apparent effort. Near Newfoundland's shores dolphins can be observed leaping for joy.

> At higher speeds the animals usually "porpoise" (leap from the water while breathing). For no apparent reason save exuberance, they often leap twenty feet out of the water, performing spins and somersaults. Because of their spectacular aerobatics, Newfoundlanders dubbed them "jumpers."[11]

We are fascinated by dolphins—and no wonder! They are star performers at aquariums who leap and splash with elegance and grace. They are warmblooded creatures who have such an advanced echolocation system that they have been recruited and studied by the U.S. Navy. Some of them also have brains that are larger than their human counterpart. In his fascinating book *A Dolphin Summer* Gerald Gormley muses about the large brains possessed by dolphins and wonders what keeps those advanced brains occupied. Because their mastery of the ocean environment is so complete, it would seem they might "have other fish to fry."

Without having to draw anthropocentric conclusions, we humans might well learn something about the joy of living from these exuberant mammals. In the times of our rejoicing, our hearts, too, need to leap with joy.

A Dolphin Date Book

Since dolphins never miss an opportunity to leap for joy, they are fitting creatures to remind us to celebrate life. You can use this date book as a starting point to list significant birthdays, anniversaries not to be missed:

January:_____

February:_____

March:_____

April:_____

May:_____

June:_____

July:_____

August:_____

September:_____

October:_____

November:_____

December:_____

Joyful Dolphin Prayer

Great Source of all being,
    we are immersed in your sea of existence.
Like the playful dolphins
    I rejoice in our course through the tides of life.
Today, I bring to mind_____, whom I love
    and the celebration of_____.

(Pause with the image; savor it; contemplate the person and event.)

Blessed be this day.
    Blessed be this beloved companion.
Blessed be memories of sacred moments.
    My heart surges for joy for such a gracious occasion.
This blessed event and the memories it holds
    stirs up the waters of life into a froth of beauty.

Blessed by the deep moments of significance
    that chart our passage through the currents of life.
Blessed be! Glory! Praise!
    Thanks for this date of jubilee!
My heart leaps and knows no bounds!

Image: Dolphins, their fins breaking the ocean's surface and then leaping high out of the water. Join your joy to theirs.

Journal: I treasure this special day for it means...

LEVIATHAN

What are submarines' surfacing
    compared with yours?
Their frail periscope skims along
    and their huge steel bodies
    rising up, dispersing frothy rivulets.
But once surfaced, they float flat-nosed,
    like the Monitor or Merrimac,
    deathly steel tubes bobbing in the water.

But you, awesome Leviathan,
    come bursting out with thunder,
    hurling upwards in your mighty breach.
Walls of water are turned to spray
    from your cyclonic fury,
    your immense hulk airborne.
Turning and twisting in a grand gyration,
    your ferocity crashes down in exclamation!

Whales of all species are indeed the exclamation point of the seas. A magnificent creature like the humpback whale, weighing some forty to fifty tons, will seek out human company. Their raw, untamed power is balanced by a gentle amiability. In a friendly and inquisitive fashion, these whales will sometimes sidle up to a boat and eye the occupants with a gentle gaze. This despite the fact that only humans and killer whales have made themselves their mortal enemies.

SOUNDS FOR REJOICING TIMES

Whales exclaim "I am here!" not only in their tremendous breaching out of the water but also in song. Jacques Cousteau describes the humpbacks as a mighty choir:

> A thousand different sounds, each one individually audible
> to the human ear. The timbre, the volume and the frequency
> present an almost infinite variety...truly polyphonic, an
> ensemble of voices.... A few of the men aboard the Curlew
> were of the opinion that the whales might be making noise
> for the sheer joy of making noise. And yet, not even the
> birds sing entirely without reason.[12]

Is not the joy of existence proclaimed by the singing and the
breaching of the whales, by the thunder of horses' hooves, as
well as by the flutter of the tiniest hummingbird? At their sight
and sound, are we not moved to exclaim, "Holy!"? Rabbi Heschel
wrote of the glory of existence,

> Just to be is a blessing. Just to live is holy![13]

Adding to that, St. Augustine of Hippo, in the fifth century,
proclaimed that the beauty all around us bears witness to its source:

> Question the beauty of the earth,
> the beauty of the seas,
> the beauty of the wide air encompassing you,
> the beauty of the skies;
> question the arrangement of the stars,
> the sun whose brightness lights up the day,
> the moon whose splendor softens the gloom of night;
> question the living creatures that move in the waters,
> that roam upon the earth,
> that fly through the air,
> the spirit that lies hidden,
> the matter that is shown forth....
>
> Question all these.
> They will respond to you:
> "Behold and see, we are beautiful."
> Their beauty is their confession of God.
> Who made these beautiful changing things,
> if not one who is beautiful and unchanging?

PRAYING WITH THE WHALE

Leviathan, Moby Dick, "Monster" of the seas,
from the psalmist, to Melville, to whale watchers,
your presence calls our imaginations from the depths.
"Thar she blows!" Great Whale!
Thrash! Splash! Breach!
Awaken our slumbering spirits!

Great Creator of this glorious creature of the seas,
no matter how deep our waters,
no matter how murky our days,
let us break the surface of ordinary time,
for "Just to be is a blessing!"

Image: The great humpback rising out of the ocean in glory and splendor. Lift up your heart to God and give praise for such glory.

Journal: I am grateful for tiny blessings like...as well as huge ones like...

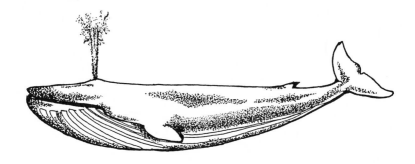

Chapter Eight

Praying with the Swan and Albatross,
Hummingbird
and Monarch Butterfly

FLIGHT OF FANCY TIMES

Too seldom do we take flights of fancy. Having mastered the art of flying, we have lost the thrill of flight. We wait in long lines at airports to be ushered through chutes into steel tubes. We can fly from New York to Los Angeles and never see anything more than the seat ahead of us. In some sense, this condensed travel impoverishes our imaginations and diminishes our sense of adventure and wonder.

It was not always so. Beryl Markham was a bush pilot of the 1930s who flew open-cockpit planes in Africa. She glided into wild places where sometimes only a cloud of elephants' dust served as a landing marker. The shrill howls of hyenas often drowned out the whine of her engine as she taxied for takeoff. The bush at the jungle's edge was her daily airdrome.

She was the first person to fly solo from England eastward across the Atlantic. Ernest Hemingway, after reading of her flying exploits in her book *West with the Night*, said that her lyrical writing made him feel like "a carpenter with words." Of her flying, Markham wrote:

> I have lifted my plane from the Nairobi airport for perhaps a thousand flights and I have never felt her wheels glide from the earth into the air without knowing the uncertainty and the exhilaration of firstborn adventure.[14]

Out of this sense of adventure in darkest Africa, she dared to dream and imagine something more—a transoceanic journey, a flight of fancy.

A NIGHT ADVENTURE

Just once, in the Yucatan jungle, I felt what she had

experienced a thousand times. We had disembarked from the Russian cruise ship Odessa in Cozumel. An optional side trip was offered to the ancient Mayan ruins in the heart of the Yucatan jungles. We could go by bus or by plane. I remembered that a friend had made the trip some years before and had strongly advised against one of these modes of transportation. I could not remember whether the ill-advised way was the plane or the bus. I chose to fly. In retrospect, the advice probably was against the plane. However, I have no regrets, for my choice was a "flight of fancy."

We flew on an old DC-6 that shook, rattled and rolled. The inner insignia said Mohawk Airlines, but that airline had been extinct for many years. We didn't pay much attention to where we landed; we were all too excited to reach the Mayan ruins.

The ruins at Chitzen Itza offered a fascinating experience. We climbed the ancient pyramid, saw the deep well where human sacrifices were offered and the field where ancient games were played, in which some of the participants literally lost their heads.

We were to return to the airstrip at 4 o'clock to meet our plane, which was to pick us up and get us back to our ship for a 7:00 P.M. sailing.

We arrived at 4:00 and waited patiently for the plane's return. The wait allowed the opportunity to observe the landing field more closely. The landing strip consisted of little more than a gravel road carved out of the jungle. The only field equipment consisted of one dirty, old windsock; it looked like it had been worn by one of the first Chicago Bears at Soldier Field.

We waited as the jungle shadows lengthened. No plane. Soon, the sun dropped beneath the green perimeter. There was still no sound from the sky. Rather quickly, night pulled a black shroud over our primitive landing strip. We looked at one another in disbelief. We were marooned in a pitch-black jungle. Night sounds from unfamiliar creatures emitted from the dense foliage. Soon little knots of people formed, each brainstorming about what we were to do next. The darkness challenged our imaginations.

One of the most pragmatic suggestions was that we should build a fire so the pilot could find us. We gathered wood from the forest and built the largest bonfire we could and then waited some more. Finally, in a silence broken only by the strange jungle noises, we heard the drone of the ancient DC-6. A few minutes later, in he came, guided by the light of our fire. He taxied over, kept the engines running, and we were hurriedly ushered aboard. Then he taxied to the very end of the strip, turned, revved up the engines and roared down the bumpy tarmac. As we lifted off, the fronds of desert trees seemed to wave to us right outside the window. The bottom of the plane lightly swished their leaves. It was that close. Back on the ship, a retired Navy man remarked, "I spent World War II on a carrier in the Pacific; I never had a more exciting takeoff than the one today from the jungle."

We escaped the Yucatan because we could imagine a solution. Beryl Markham pioneered aviation because she too dared to imagine a new way to go. She dared to dream and take a flight of fancy.

The Ancient Flyers

The exhilaration of flight! We take it for granted, yet only in our age have humans experienced such a marvelous ascent. What of the true veterans of flight? They have skimmed the earth and roamed the heavens for millions of years! Their grace, their skills, their own "radar systems," their beauty in flight can stimulate our imaginations and enliven our dreams. Consider the swan, the albatross, the hummingbird, the butterfly. Let them accompany you on flights of fancy.

Praying with the Swan and the Albatross

Both the albatross and the whooper swan might be called the *Concordes* of jet-set birds! Actually the supersonic Concorde's curving fuselage is patterned on a swan's neck. Together, these two winged creatures possess more than a share of the high-flying aircraft's qualities.

The albatross is enshrined as a legend in the "Ryme of the Ancient Mariner." Its wingspan measures as much as twelve feet, and its life span approximates human age limits. It can fly around the world, traveling as much as 35,000 miles in three months! These birds are able to soar atop the thermals. They alight on land only to breed. The sky is their domain, the sea their table, the earth their nuptial bed.

The whooper swan possesses all the grace and elegant beauty of other swans and is a true transcontinental flyer. According to the *Guiness Book of Remarkable Animals*, a flock of these birds has been tracked on a radar screen flying at 27,000 feet! This is just slightly below the jet-stream where winds of incredible ferocity are encountered.

Both the albatross and the swan gloriously soar almost beyond the bounds of our imaginations.

My Spirit Like the Swan

Who could imagine a bird as high as the heavens
or a winged adventurer circling the earth?

High-soaring Spirit of God,
I celebrate the wondrous creatures
that flow from your flights of fancy.
I imagine within me a swan of arched beauty,
a feathered wisp riding the crest of all my desires.

Call her beauty.
Call her glory.
Call her hope against hope.

Can I imagine myself flying farther
than anyone else would dream?

Yes! There is an energy that moves me
beyond a reflection of so small a self.
I rejoice in the divine dynamism
that shakes loose my winged human spirit,
that empowers my imagination
to far exceed what others cast as my lot.
I am more than the sum of my parts,
more than dust in the wind.

From clay to cloud, my spirit soars,
sailing up, surmounting petty cabined fears,
soaring up beyond narcissistic mirrors.
With joy, I bless the day.
With peace, I greet the night.
With serene grace, I praise my creator.
With ease, I fly toward the stars.
There is no limit beyond my dreams.

Image: The majestic, soaring swan above the clouds. Pray your hopes and dreams...

Journal: My imagination leads me to soar toward...

Praying with the Hummingbird

The hummingbird is the tiniest of birds, yet it is a creature of immense energy. It hovers, darts, ascends, descends and even flys backwards. Like the bee, it feeds on nectar from flowers and must continually be energized to enable it to sustain an incredible tempo clocked as high as eighty-five wingbeats per second! Despite its frenetic activity, when it alights on the most fragile stem, its landing is so precise and delicate that the branch does not bend nor move.

> Who could imagine so much
> residing in so little?

The Apaches believe the hummingbird to be a special messenger. When it hovers near, it calls us to pay attention. As you consider this winged harbinger, what is its message for you?

A Hummingbird Prayer

Spirit of our highest aspirations and deepest dreams,
    in a flight of fancy mood,
    would that I could see my world
    as a hummingbird does:

    I would take precious moments to sniff the flowers,
        tapping into every precious variety.
    I would hover over the fragrance of life.
    I would be mobile in my imagination,
unencumbered and alert to each of life's tiny pleasures,
    each dear moment worth its weight in gold.

    Boredom would find no domicile
for earth is a dwelling surrounded with gardens,
    banked high with flowers.

I would seek to be continually energized by your fragrant grace.
    I would pull up and away from sour, rancid days
    and descend to the very point of my heart's desire.

    Reveling in the splendor of each petal,
    each golden branch; my rest would be intense,
    my flight fluid and graceful.

An artisan of flight, a harrier rising straight up,
    pulled up and away again and again
    toward my pursuit of bliss.

Image: In a flight of fancy mood, see your world as the hummingbird does...

Journal: The message of the hummingbird for me is...

PRAYING WITH THE MONARCH BUTTERFLY

Insects can only grow by making a new skin beneath the old one and discarding the top one...the new skin develops a number of folds which can expand like a concertina, opening out when the old skin is discarded.

George Ordist, *The Year of the Butterfly*

The monarch butterfly is regal indeed. The sun has never shone more resplendently through any prism than it does through the brilliant orange wings of the monarch. Each bright wing panel is outlined in black like a great stained glass window framed by lead tracings. But unlike an inert window, the monarch has come a long way, and will travel a long way to show forth its splendor.

The magnificent monarch is the final result of a caterpillar having gone through several different mutations before its final emergence as a winged beauty. After this metamorphosis some of these delicate butterflies are capable of migrating over two thousand miles, all the way to Mexico!

> Who could ever imagine a worm
> turning into a butterfly and
> then embarking on an odyssey?
> Does a divine imagination permeate
> every cell of our reality?

As the odyssey continues, some new butterflies are hatched along the route. As a result, some migrate back to a place from which they never came! Their flight sometimes takes them over tall buildings and even over three thousand feet high mountains.

Hovering over a flower, their wings are like those of angels, their inner process gives witness to the wisdom of the deep-down possibilities of transformation!

When we recognize the mystery of transformation, we grow in wisdom. There is an ancient Sufi dialog that speaks to this truth:

"Wisdom," the Holy One said, "is simply the ability to recognize."

"I know that," the disciple said, "but the question is to recognize *what*?"

"Spiritual wisdom," the Holy One said, "is the ability to recognize the butterfly in a caterpillar; the eagle in an egg; the saint in a sinner."[15]

Transformation from deep within: do we forget that this is possible for humans too? The emerging butterfly goes through stages of letting go. Perhaps, we delude ourselves by thinking that we can be deeply transformed by adding on. Actors endure layers of makeup, and they are surrounded by props before their drama ushers forth. Football heroes are padded, jerseyed and have their heads bottled in plastic before they go out on the field. The surgeon scrubs, gowns and is masked before her gloved hand guides the scalpel. The fighter pilot is zipped up and visored before being sealed in his plexiglass cocoon. We add on, pile up, dress up, accumulate in the hope of being transformed. In the human situation, change and its subsequent activity seems to result from added equipment. Even in death, we are painted and padded.

But for the butterfly, change and flight soar from within! They erupt from some deep-down cellular code. A crawly, creepy worm breaks out of itself several times and then wraps itself in a mummy's tomb soon to become a royal portal. When the monarch comes forth, has the world ever seen so great a flutter?

Is there something in me that waits accordion-like to be unfolded? Are my languid movements and moods the brooding times for new adventures? Do I possess in the depths of my sacred imagination the potential to be transformed by letting go, by flights of fancy, by risking change?

An even deeper question: Are sickness or even death cocoons hiding unexpected life?

PRAYER OF AN EMERGING SELF

Marvelous Creator of the butterfly,
 set loose in me the energy of new creation.
Move me out of self, out of self, out of self, out of self,
 into chrysalis and beyond.

Seed my imagination.
 Lift up my wings.
Drawn by unknown scents and different destinies,
 let me rise, rise, rise
 out of the depths of chrysalis crisis.
Even out of death in all its forms.

Image: The monarch butterfly emerging, taking wing, being drawn to a beautiful garden. From this beauty, I pray...

Journal: I imagine I could....

PRAYING WITH THE MONARCH, CRANES AND CREATURES
A GUIDED MEDITATION

For this guided meditation, assume a relaxed position. Do a few deep breaths and sense your body relaxing. When you can feel the circulation in your body, you are beginning to relax. This will be a journey into your sacred imagination. (If you have a tape recorder, record the text below with pauses and let that be your guide.)

Imagine:

You are sitting in a darkened room. There is a projection screen in front of you. The first image of a slide show is projected there: it shows a blue sky with a few puffy clouds. Be present to it; let it relax you.

You will now be shown a series of slides of various creatures. Just observe and enjoy, no analysis. Let go of words, and let these images imprint themselves on your own imagination:

... a whooping crane dancing, with its red-capped head, white feathers tipped in black

... a sandhill crane, red-capped, brownish grey body, lying with its long spindly legs trailing

... a snail barely moving across a path

... a silver salmon leaping up a waterfall

... a grizzly reaching out a paw to catch the salmon

... a wolf howling

... wild geese forming a "V" high in the sky

... the saguaro cactus standing tall in the desert sun

... the desert tortoise resting beneath the cactus

... the eagle flying high in the sky

... the rain forest with its green ferns, reeds and overarching trees

... the bluish green waters of the Caribbean—you diving and peering at the strange and exotic creatures of a coral reef

... the mighty redwoods towering above you

... your favorite domestic pet

... a cat stretching

... a golden retriever swimming back to shore

... the ancient mariner and the albatross

... a horse running free

... a dolphin skimming the surface

... a whale breaching

... a swan above the clouds

... a hummingbird sipping nectar from a flower

... an orange and black monarch butterfly in flight

Now imagine you have a book on your lap. It is your autobiography. See your name on it. But there is a blank rectangle below your name.

On a table before you are pictures identical to all the slides you have just seen. Pick out *one* that you would like to symbolize your life story. Imagine yourself pasting that picture on the cover.

Now open the book to its table of contents. There is a chapter there for each decade of your life: Chapter 1 is for age 1-10, Chapter 2 covers years 10-20, etc. Turn to the chapter that corresponds to your present decade in life. There is a creature picture there that symbolizes this decade, this immediate time span in your life. Take a peek:

What do you see?

Does the creature's image bring you joy? Are you satisfied with it? If so, gaze at it, savor it.... Or does it make you feel uneasy or even fearful? If so, is there something you can learn from this image?

Perhaps your creature is challenging you to develop a particular quality in your life—great-heartedness, freedom, faithfulness, perseverance, or even playfulness.... Or might the image signify a transit point in your journey?

You may like to change it. It's your story and you can, you know. If you wish to replace it, recall now the images of the creatures you saw before. Pick out the one you want.... Now take its picture and paste it at the beginning of your current chapter. Gaze at if for awhile and enjoy it....

Close the book for now; you can always open it up again at another time. Another image may suggest itself.

Journal: Praying with creatures leads me...

Notes

1. Christopher Bamford and William Marsh, *Celtic Christianity, Ecology and Holiness* (Rochester, VT: Lindsfarne Press, Traditions International, 1982), p. 106.

2. Michael Meade, *Men and the Water of Life* (New York: Harper Collins, 1993), book flap.

3. Bob Holmes, "Beyond Beauty" column, *U.S. News and World Report*, November 30, 1992, p. 67.

4. CRS pamphlet, P.O. Box 17090, Baltimore, Md., 21298.

5. Marsilio Ficino, quoted by Thomas Moore, *Care of the Soul* (New York: Harper Collins, 1992), p. 172.

6. Meister Eckhart, from Matthew Fox, *Meditations, A Centering Book* (Santa Fe: Bear & Co., 1982), p. 14.

7. Dr. Adair Alspach, quoted by Geoffrey Tomb, "These Real Corporate Cats Reign Over the Workplace," *Miami Herald*, March 10, 1991.

8. Barbara Berliner, *Book of Answers* (New York: Prentice Hall).

9. Walter W. Winget, "Letters," *U.S. News and World Report*, June 3, 1995.

10. John and Caitlin Matthews, *The Little Book of Celtic Wisdom* (Rockport, MA: Element, 1993), p. 17.

11. Gerald Gormley, *A Dolphin Summer* (New York: Taplinger Publishing, 1985), p. 21.

12. Jacques-Yves Cousteau, trans. J.F. Bernard, *The Whale, Mighty Monarch of the Sea* (New York: Doubleday & Co., 1972), p. 113.

13. Abraham Heschel, *Conservative Judaism*, 25, Fall, 1970, p. 81.

14. Beryl Markham, *West with the Night* (San Francisco: North Point Press, 1983), p. 9.

15. A poem from the Sufi tradition, quoted by Joan Chittister, "Yesterday's Dangerous Vision," *Sojourners Magazine*, July 1987, p. 181.